Miss Matched
AT MIDLIFE

Rebecca Brockway

Miss Matched

AT MIDLIFE

——— *Dating Episodes of a Middle-Aged Woman* ———

Rebecca Brockway

NORTH LOOP BOOKS | MINNEAPOLIS, MN

North Loop Books
322 First Avenue N, 5th floor
Minneapolis, MN 55401
612.455.2294
www.NorthLoopBooks.com

ISBN-13: 978-1-63413-888-8
LCCN: 2016906045

Distributed by Itasca Books

Cover photo by Mel Bradshaw Photography
Cover Design by Alan Pranke
Typeset by Biz Cook & C. Tramell
Clip art from Shutterstock

Printed in the United States of America

To Pops and my kids

Contents

Foreword

FOR THE FIRST TIME IN US HISTORY, singles of all ages comprise the majority of the country's population. National polls report that 48 percent of New York's citizens are unmarried and living alone. In today's modern world, "grown-up" dating is a necessary skill; yet, as most singles that have dated at midlife will tell you, help is needed!

Following the collapse of a first marriage or an extended relationship, many of my clients reenter the dating pool in their forties, fifties, or sixties. Often they express dismay over the whole ordeal: "I hate this!" or "How do I say no to somebody I'm not interested in?" or "What are the 'secret rules' and hazards of Internet dating?" This is especially true of women, who initiate more divorces than men, and who often despair over finding a guy they like who's willing to do the work of a relationship.

Enter Rebecca Brockway, author of *Miss Matched at Midlife: Dating Episodes of a Middle-Aged Woman*. She's here to entertain and inform, as she offers us her incredible real-life dating experiences.

In her quest to discover authentic love after divorce, Rebecca went on at least 150 first dates, but she never gave up on love. Her book is for individuals who have conscientiously employed the common-day wisdom of "how to land a mate after forty-five," yet have continued to come up "mismatched."

As a therapist, author, and frontline relationship and sexuality stalwart for the last forty-one years, I heartily agree with Rebecca's conclusions and tips, and you'll enjoy seeing how she followed (and occasionally *didn't* follow) her own rules. Even more, it is great fun to read about the hard-earned lessons that have turned Rebecca into a self-taught dating guru. As I progressed from one true tale to the next, I thought: *How can she top this story?* Yet, often, Rebecca does just that. Each episode is a prize.

Rebecca indulged in what-the-heck-sex, learned how to tell a scam artist from an earnest good guy, experienced the mystical power of stilettos, and discovered when to absolutely pull the plug after the first date. *Miss Matched at Midlife* is composed of twenty-nine unbarred windows into dating, brought to you by a courageous woman going where millions have gone before, and generous enough to take us along for the ride.

In today's marketplace, there's not enough written about managing the job of parenthood while trying to incorporate being a single, dating parent at the same time. How does one deal with the inevitable embarrassments of dating life, integrated into sack lunches and homework? I like how Rebecca attempts to find balance between dates and her children—and I admire her extraordinary honesty when she gets it completely wrong.

A lecturer on male-female relationships, Allison Armstrong is one of my favorite teachers. She says that too many women become "frog farmers"; they try to shape a "wrong-choice man" into a "great-choice man." This often arises out of a sense of lack, as if there aren't enough male candidates. The rationale goes: once you've snagged a guy, you'd better hold on and not assert your own needs or personality too much. Rebecca has discovered there is no shortage of single middle-aged men—it just takes an investment of time and effort to sort through them, to find one who's a "prince."

Everything becomes less scary the more we practice, and so it is with dating. After reading *Miss Matched at Midlife*, you will have vicariously experienced a fascinating array of first dates—and a fair number of relationships—leaving you wiser and stronger in understanding our shared human drive for romantic life partners.

Dr. Keith Witt is a clinical psychologist, writer, and teacher. Dr. Witt has authored five books, including *Integral Mindfulness*, *The Attuned Family*, and *The Gift of Shame*. He and his company, Integral Life, offer the popular *Loving Completely* audio relationship course. Dr. Witt has lectured widely across the country, on topics such as intimacy, sexuality, psychotherapy, and integral psychology. Find out more about Dr. Keith Witt at drkeithwitt.com.

Fish to Fry

ONCE UPON A TIME I WAS A BRIDE. For many years afterwards, I was a wife. I would like to be a bride—and a wife—again someday.

My wedding day: February 11, 1989. A bout of stomach flu threatened to deter me, but I wasn't about to let a virus spoil my big day. I was thirty-one years old and convinced it was time I became a grown-up. The groom was still boyishly handsome at twenty-eight. My gown was a dramatic production representative of the '80s and had been featured on the cover of *Brides* magazine. Off the shoulder, with a fitted waist, full skirt, and decorative rosettes, my wedding dress would have made Scarlett O'Hara swoon. In it, I was the quintessential Southern (California) belle. The gown's fabric was heavy brocade in ivory—not white. Traditionally speaking, I was not worthy of white. I had been living with my fiancé, Mickey— "shacking up," as my father would say—for over a year.

At home following the festivities, I peeled my dress and undergarments from my body. They'd felt like painful scabs. I loosened my gown and let it tumble to my ankles. Piece by piece, my bridal finery fell to the living room floor: the merry widow (an ominously named item for a merry bride's wardrobe), stiff petticoat, and veil. Contrary to appearances, my abandoned clothes were not the pell-mell trail of a newly married woman eager to join her husband in their marriage bed. I had left my wedding garments where they fell because I was too ill to pick them up. I was much too sick for sex. During the reception, I'd kept a bottle of Pepto-Bismol close by—taking a swig as needed—a queasy consort's substitute for the customary glass of celebratory champagne. My new husband assured me I'd feel better once we set out for Lake Tahoe the next morning.

Bumping along in an old Ford pickup did nothing to soothe my nausea. Our second night as newlyweds was spent at the Gunn House Hotel in Sonora, California. By that time, Mickey had come down with the virus as well, but I had mostly recovered. I crawled beneath the crisp white sheets and floral duvet that adorned the antique bed, and ate a Baby Ruth candy bar I'd purchased at the front desk. Green around the gills, Mickey lay beside me and moaned.

The next day we drove the final leg of our journey. We checked into a shabby Lake Tahoe motel room that Mickey had reserved as part of our honeymoon package. He had such fond memories of the place. He and his buddies had stayed there on a long-ago guys-only ski trip. Back then, they'd been a group of drunken college-aged dudes, content with their sordid quarters, which sported orange shag carpet and an array of black velvet paintings. My favorite: a scrawny, sad-eyed kitten that hung above the timeworn double bed. When he unlocked the door to our room, my husband exclaimed, "It looks exactly the same!" I sighed. It wasn't how I'd envisioned our honeymoon love nest.

The following afternoon we visited the town of Brockway, California. Mickey snapped a picture of me standing in the snow under a sign that read *Brockway*: my maiden name. Yet, for most of our time in Tahoe, I lay on the carpet outside the tiny bathroom, which was equipped with a pocket door—reminiscent of a train privy—and offered moral support to Mickey as he purged from both ends. We didn't consummate our legal bond until the fifth day of marital bliss. We'd had ourselves a rocky start. An omen, perhaps?

On our wedding day, my husband had married *me*. He'd taken *me* as his wife. He'd arrived at the marriage feast with fewer expectations. For better or worse, he wanted *me*.

But I hadn't felt the same way. Being Mickey's wife was not enough. I had bigger fish to fry. My marriage had been the springboard for what I really wanted: to be a mother. Even before their births, it was my children I was married to.

Although it was a top priority in my life, Mickey and I hadn't discussed children before we tied the knot. We hadn't considered what we would do if children didn't come easily for us. Ill-equipped for what lay ahead, we exchanged "I dos."

Mickey and I quit birth control. A year passed. I had exploratory surgery. Things didn't look good—my fallopian tubes were severely scarred. My doctor suggested we try another route. For the next three years, we commuted from Santa Barbara to LA to undergo a total of six cycles of in vitro fertilization financed with the money I earned as a grocery checker. My embryos didn't stick. None of them ever did. The unsuccessful medical procedures taxed our financial, physical, and emotional reserves.

After years of struggling to conceive—and an early-term miscarriage—I decided Mickey and I should adopt. I had led the way with our infertility treatments, and it was *I* who spearheaded the adoptions. It was *I* who took the reins.

Mickey and I moved from Santa Barbara to San Luis Obispo. Over the next ten years, we brought home four babies. Each adoption was a laborious yet rewarding experience. We loved our children. But my single-minded determination to become a mom had taken a destructive toll on my marriage. The act of seeking my children and gathering them to me had necessitated my total focus. I chose the full-time occupation of motherhood over being my husband's wife.

It's generally assumed that couples fight about sex or money. My spouse and I fought about adoption. To me, adoption was an exciting adventure and a noble quest. But to Mickey, adoption was an overwhelming and frightening unknown. Before each child was sought, I begged and cried until he finally gave in with a reluctant "yes." My friends said I should be grateful I had "won," but going to battle over a privilege that came easily to most women seemed unjust. I thought Mickey was cruel to punish me for wanting—*needing*—children. I don't think he realized that my adopted babies were lifesavers upon my sea of heartbreak.

A cautious man, Mickey was motivated by financial security, and adoption was an expensive proposition with no guarantees. He wanted us to stick to a ten-year plan of lying low (modest spending), staying put (no home buying or selling), and maintaining the status quo (taking no chances). I tried to convince him that life was a glorious crapshoot that petitioned us to step out and take a calculated risk—*to live a little!* Mickey tried to convince me that life was fraught with peril and governed by money. His motto was "better safe than sorry . . ." We had little patience, or compassion, for each other's point of view.

On our wedding day, Mickey had married *me*—but "me" was

more headstrong wife than he had bargained for, and I came to believe I'd picked the short end of the stick for a husband. Neither of us was acutely aware of who we'd married until it was too late.

I want to try my hand at being a wife again. I view the bond of marriage as a sacred thing not to be trifled with. I want to enter into a partnership where we regard ourselves as equals—not in all areas, of course—but in the way we value and support one another's ambitions and emotional needs. I want to build a life with a man. I look forward to a practical, romantic, and *adventurous* pairing. That is the reason why, at this stage of my life, I continue to actively date. If I were to give up—throw in the towel—I might never realize my dream. My life experience has taught me that perseverance does win the race. And that's what I'll do.

Wild One

I HAVE NEVER RUN WITH THE BULLS IN PAMPLONA. I have never dined on a deadly fugu fish. I have never bungee jumped off the world's highest bridge. I've never even jumped off the high dive at the Y. Yet, I'm a thrill seeker. In the past nine years, since my divorce at age forty-eight, I've been on at least 150 first dates.

One hundred and fifty first dates is *a lot*. The vast majority of them have been duds. So why did I keep accepting these invitations? Why did I continue to contact men on online dating sites? Let me share a story that illustrates my personal philosophy about getting what one wants in life.

Mickey's best friend and his wife had a son two years before Mickey and I adopted our first child. Then, the couple struggled to have another baby. She'd get pregnant easily but miscarry early on. Losing babies was heartbreaking for the couple, as losing babies always is. Over the course of six years, Mickey and I had adopted three newborns, so I suggested to our friends that they consider adoption. The wife told me if somebody left an infant on her doorstep, she would gladly parent, but she didn't want to put forth the effort to adopt. The couple never had another baby. Mickey and I eventually adopted a total of four—none of whom had been left swaddled and abandoned on our stoop.

It would be an exceptional occurrence for a desperate couple to discover a needy infant on their front step. Likewise, it would be an exceptional occurrence for a single middle-aged woman to discover her ideal romantic match by doing absolutely nothing to facilitate such a discovery. Locating one's mate at midlife rarely occurs through a serendipitous encounter. Most of the time, assistance is needed. Although miraculous stories of found babies and found love do exist, such tales are the exception. Most of the time we need to work hard and persevere to get what we want. Most of the time we have to step outside our comfort zone and risk failure to reach an important goal.

Miss Matched at Midlife is not a manual on "how to land a man after age forty-five." My book is a collection of the tales and the wisdom I acquired throughout my time dating online and in "real life." None of my experiences were staged. I did not set out to write a book and then schedule dates in order to gather material. I have always dated with a singular goal in mind: to discover authentic love at midlife. My approach was pretty simple. I figured if I wanted to find a boyfriend I should start by dating boys (aka men). Maybe I should have run with the bulls instead. But in a way, I have. My journey has been a wild one.

When I first reentered single life after seventeen years of marriage, I purchased a month's subscription to Match.com. I supposed one month would be sufficient time to discover Mr. Right. I also believed that single middle-aged men would vie to scoop me up because I came with a delightful added bonus: my four young children. I was a wee naive.

Based on number of subscribers, Pew Research Center has determined Match.com, Plenty Of Fish, and eHarmony to be among the top dating sites. Each touts its unique approach and stellar results. Here's a brief rundown of the sites I've used.

Match.com is my favorite destination for seeking love online. A basic three-month membership can be purchased for less than seventy-five dollars. The site is straightforward, easy to access and utilize, and there are many male subscribers in my area. However, there appears to be a growing number of profiles posted on Match.com that do not include the man's photo. This leads me to suspect that men who are already in established relationships troll the site. There are also a smattering of fake profiles posted by scam artists intent on stealing the hearts and money of inexperienced female subscribers. Familiarity with Internet dating has taught me to spot counterfeit profiles (more on that later), and I steer clear. If a man seems too good to be true, he may be. Dater beware.

Plenty Of Fish is free to join, and very user friendly. If a member wants to log on to engage in amiable chitchat with another subscriber, this is the place to do it. Most male subscribers I've encountered are enthusiastic participants in chatty one-line exchanges and how-do-you-dos. POF once lacked a reputable image, but no longer. I've recently read an endorsement for POF posted on a professional dating coach's website. I used to secure the majority of my dates from Plenty Of Fish, but I have tired of the site's overly casual climate.

eHarmony has been a disappointment. The site claims: *Our bold, scientific approach to matching means more quality dates with deeply compatible singles that truly understand you.* I subscribed to eHarmony because of its reputation for being a dating site designed for individuals serious about discovering a viable partner. I assumed that eHarmony would prove a more effective matchmaker than either Match.com or Plenty Of Fish. I was wrong. A basic three-month membership costs about $120. It delivers little besides a beautiful profile layout, reminiscent of a professional scrapbook page, and an insightful customized personality assessment titled "The Book of You." In spite of its fancy presentation and "bold, scientific approach," eHarmony's method of matchmaking was more hassle than helpful, and the site paired me with numerous men who resided outside of my area.

To all naysayers of Internet dating: according to a study commissioned by eHarmony, more than 33 percent of American marriages today get their start online. Though not foolproof, Internet dating sites are convenient modern-day matchmakers for busy singles. A credible dating site is a tool that will help you build a romantic relationship, be it a date, a boyfriend, or a husband. By the same token, a hammer is a tool that will build you a house, but only if you pick it up each day and wield it over and over until you've constructed your dream.

While it's fun to window-shop for a mate online, it is exceedingly difficult to determine one's ideal match from a handful of photos and a few words on a computer screen. The only way you will ever know if a man is a suitable match is to transition from cyberspace to the reality of a coffee shop, a barstool, or the beach. These are seemingly common destinations that may offer you the thrill of a lifetime.

Dating after forty-five is not easy. I wrote *Miss Matched at Midlife* because it's important that single middle-aged women understand they are not alone in their dating disappointments, frustrations, and mishaps. A woman can diligently implement everything a "how to land a man" manual tells her, yet even so, sometimes calamity will step in and take over. And sometimes grace.

My hard-earned dating advice? A safety harness and protective headgear are recommended. Oh yes—*and* a matador's cape.

The Strange, the Bad & the Ugly

What Men's Online Profiles *Really* Tell Us

Middle-Aged Men's Photos Decoded:

Big mustache	Stuck in the 1980s. Wears tighty-whities.
Ratty ponytail	Smarmy (e.g., late comedian George Carlin).
Earring(s)	Old wannabe hipster (e.g., actor Harrison Ford).
Posed with his lifted truck or luxury car	Immature and insecure. Small penis likely.
Posted photos of his pit bull	Antagonist. Believes nothing tempts romance like an argument (or a mauling).

No posted photos	Married.
Blurry photos	He's on the lam. Check post office for in-focus mug shot.
Shirtless selfies in bathroom mirror	Marky Mark impersonator.
All photos include his children/pets	Emotionally unavailable to outsiders.
Raucous party photos	Ex–frat boy/bad boy. Big penis.
Posted his baby pic	Seeks mother figure. Boob-man.
Neck or knuckle tattoos	Ex-con/gang member. No car. Sleeps on air mattress.
Posed with his buddies in a multitude of exotic locations	Lonely as hell.
Poker face	Bad teeth or badass. Both likely.
Posted numerous photos of his extraordinary life	Narcissist.
Posted glamour shot of his jumbo-sized Hog (Harley)	Piglet-sized penis.
Claims he is 57. His photos look like he's 67.	He's 67.
George Clooney look-alike	Too hot to handle.
Woody Allen look-alike	Brilliant. Neurotic. Alleged pervert.
Posted pics of schmaltzy Precious Moments quotes	Desperate.
Wears cowboy hat in all his photos	Bald cowboy.
Wears multicolored argyle vest and baggy shorts	Moonlights as circus clown.
Wears wedding ring	Busted!

Middle-Aged Men's Written Profiles Decoded:

Typed his profile in all upper-case or all lowercase letters	Writes ransom notes for a living.
Recorded no data in his personal information section	Married.
Claims he's "passionate" about life	Thinks he's dynamite in the sack.
Claims he's a "bad boy" behind closed doors	Seeks sexual conquests/spankings.
Lists his ten favorite bands, all of them obscure	Snobbish bore.
Lives on his boat	Seeks no responsibility.
He's 55 years old, never married, no children	Lives on his boat.
He's 55 years old and seeks women 18–36	Dirty old man.
Claims to have met a lot of crazy women on the dating site	Bipolar.
Seeks friend/lover/life partner	Old hippie. Seeks free love.
His first-date suggestion: a walk on the beach	Ambivalent. Cheapskate.
He "lives, laughs, loves"	Conformist. Wears a windbreaker. Drives a Yaris.
Doesn't disclose his income	Poor as dirt.
Says he's trying to quit smoking	Smoker.
Cigar aficionado	Pretentious smoker. Tea Party affiliate.
Never drinks	Recovering alcoholic.

Drinks regularly	Drinks constantly.
Handsome earnest widower who prefers older women	Scam artist.
Separated/divorced less than one year	Basket case.
Divorced twenty-five years	Committed bachelor. Soaks dried beans overnight for next day's meal.
Seems normal	Fair to middling chance he is.
Seeks women "friends"	Liar.
Claims he'll "try anything once"	Opportunist. Seeks kinky sex.
Seeks a "fun" girl	Seeks an "easy" girl.
Claims he'll treat his date like a "queen"	He'll play Henry VIII opposite Anne Boleyn if his date's not a fun girl.

What-the-Heck-Sex

FIVE-YEAR-OLD MAX—THE YOUNGEST OF MY BROOD—sat with me on our front porch. I busied myself with scooping the slimy fibers and seeds from his Halloween pumpkin as Greg drove up and parked his truck across the street. He climbed out and closed the door. I got a good look at him then. He was handsome. Handsome enough, anyway: tall, lean runner's body, with short curly hair going gray. He wore khakis, a linen short-sleeved button-down shirt, and flip-flops. Clean-shaven Greg looked like a *GQ* surfer. He'd come by to pick me up for our first date. This was back in my early days of postdivorce dating. Nowadays, I don't let a man I've recently met online come to my house to pick me up. This practice has less to do with safety concerns and more to do with not wanting to be stuck with an ill-matched suitor.

I was intent on finishing the messy seed removal, and to do so, I employed the aid of a tarnished serving spoon. Carving would have to wait. I stood and wiped my hands on an old dish towel. I extended my right one and Greg reluctantly shook it.

"You've been slimed!" I said.

Greg laughed. We were off to a good start.

I set my son's hollow pumpkin to the side and gathered the newspapers I'd laid out to collect the squash's entrails. In stark contrast to the smell of fresh pumpkin, I detected the savory aroma of barbecued beef mingled with the pungent smell of cannabis. I glanced over at the yellow two-story house next door where my four college-aged neighbors lived. Three of the young men were on their front porch grilling hamburgers and smoking whatnot. They looked over at me, too—no doubt curious about the goings-on of their new neighbor. I raised my hand in greeting.

"Hi there!" I hollered. Two of the boys ignored me. One of them returned my hello. He was the sweet one of the bunch. When I had moved in two months before, he had brought me a welcome-to-the-neighborhood card. For the life of me, I couldn't remember his name.

I called through the screen door to inform my fourteen-year-old daughter, Roma, I was leaving. I'd hired her to be Max's babysitter for the evening. He was the tough one. The other two kids would be easy for her to handle. Roma appeared on the other side of the door. I pulled it open.

"Honey, this is Greg. We're going out for a while, but I shouldn't be too late. You can call me if you need anything. I left money for dinner on the built-in hutch. Call Village Host Pizza. They're close by and we know them. They'll deliver. They're safe."

I was a protective mom. Yet, was I a bad parent to leave my fourteen-year-old daughter alone to babysit her three younger siblings?

The interior of Greg's Ford Explorer was tidy—no fast-food wrappers or old cardboard coffee cups—but it smelled weird, like damp gone bad and laundry detergent. Not a stench exactly, but rather a troublesome odor, spiked with the sweet smell of Tide. Greg cleared his throat. Then he cleared it again. He had a tickle.

"I've planned for us to walk on Pismo Beach," Greg said as he drove down my street. He'd placed both hands upon the steering wheel at ten and two. He wore a large field watch, and his hands were weathered and dry, in need of a good moisturizer.

"It's such a pretty afternoon. The beach sounds like a great idea!" Everybody's cheerleader: me.

Greg drove south to the small community of Pismo Beach, where a wooden boardwalk flanks the sand, and the beach is wide and clean. He parked on a narrow side street in front of a row of tiny bungalows with white picket fences. Red and pink geraniums, and wooden pelicans or sandpipers with windmill wings, were planted in each yard. Greg took a small backpack from behind the front seat and slipped it on. We walked a block to the sand, kicked off our flip-flops, and strolled along the shore until the sky grew ashen. Greg was not much of a talker, and he seemed a little uptight. But he was okay. I was glad to be on a date with him.

Greg cleared his throat. "Let's sit in the sand. I've brought us a bottle of wine."

I was impressed. Greg had put some real thought into his preparations. Most of the time a man will not invest much effort into a first date. I understand the solid reasoning behind this determination, and I agree with it. It is a risky endeavor to plan a first date that will involve more than an hour of either party's time. Once you're face-to-face with an individual you've never seen—except for the photos they've posted on a dating website—their physical looks or demeanor can be a shock. People are commonly not what they've portrayed themselves to be.

I burrowed my bare feet into the granulized warmth. I dug my hands into the sand and grabbed some. I raised my fists, opened them, and let the handfuls of sand fall between my fingers.

Greg unzipped his backpack and removed two wine glasses, wrapped in two separate kitchen towels. He opened a bottle of zinfandel and poured us each a glass. Greg cleared his throat. Maybe the wine would help ease that irritation.

Greg looked straight ahead. "You're better than I thought you'd be," he said. "Once, I met up with a woman whose online photos were beautiful. I had arranged to take her to dinner, but in person she was so fat! I told her I couldn't go through with it."

Greg had bigger balls than I did. I would always sit through a bad date, grinning and bearing it. I never wanted to hurt anybody's feelings.

"What happened then? What did she say?"

"She got mad. She said I owed her dinner."

"And?"

"I left. I wasn't going to waste my time."

Greg's behavior seemed a little harsh. His story had set me on edge. *You're better than I thought you'd be?* Was that supposed to be a compliment? Couldn't Greg have simply said he thought I was pretty? I sucked in my stomach. I didn't want to look fat. I didn't know what to say in response to Greg's odd tale.

The sun slipped from its lofty perch and came to rest on the ocean. I scanned the red horizon, resplendent with a bright splash of marinara sauce. *I must be hungry,* I thought. Greg cleared his throat.

"I don't want to drop you off just yet. Would you like to go to dinner in Pismo?"

"Yes, dinner sounds wonderful."

I was glad Greg had chosen me. I was glad he didn't think I was a waste of his time.

On only two occasions have I ever had sex on the first date. Greg was one of those. But first we went to Giuseppe's. We drank wine and ate pesto and fresh shrimp tossed with angel-hair pasta. Greg had borrowed my reading glasses to read the menu. He looked silly and endearing in my horn-rims. Greg was a bit guarded but he flashed a big smile—*the yin and the yang.* I liked him.

Following dinner, Greg drove me back to my house and I invited him in. When I unlocked the front door and opened it, I could see that the TV had been left on, the volume turned low. A pizza box sat on top of the coffee table. I lifted the lid. The box was empty except for three pieces of dry crust that had been gnawed into boomerangs. There was also a scattering of black olives—tiny spare tires—on the bottom of the box. I knew they had come from Max's pizza. Max hated olives. I peeked in on my kids. They were asleep.

We lay on my bed. I gave the okay for Greg to rub his penis on my vagina, but not to penetrate. But it was an impossible temptation for me to lie on my bed with a sexy guy who'd looked endearing in my horn-rims. My horn-rims and the wine and the beach had made me horny for him. *What the heck,* I thought. *I'm not married anymore. I can do whatever I want to. My kids are asleep and I've a handsome stranger in my bed. What's the harm? I'll figure everything out tomorrow.* The truth was, following my divorce, single men and relationships seemed much too complex to figure out at all. I didn't understand how to secure the reciprocal love I desired. Instead, I learned to numb my inhibitions, throw caution to the wind, and succumb to "what-the-heck-sex."

Early the next morning, Roma opened the door to our home's only bathroom and discovered Greg standing at the toilet, penis out, peeing a yellow stream. It had been an unfortunate encounter for both. I had meant no harm and Greg had meant no disrespect. Still, my teenage daughter had not viewed it that way. Roma interpreted Greg's presence as an overt sign I'd betrayed her. I wasn't surprised. A week earlier, Roma had informed me that I was too old for dating or new love. As far as she was concerned, it was my duty to be her sacrificial mother and nothing more. She was pissed she had to share me with her younger brothers and sister. She was pissed I divorced her father. She was pissed we didn't live on easy street. She was pissed that Greg had pissed in our toilet. Roma has never forgiven me for allowing Greg to sleep over and use the bathroom.

I loved my children, but I was guilty of needing more. Prior to Greg spending the night, I hadn't ironed out the wrinkles that accompany postdivorce romance and kids. I have serious doubts whether postdivorce wrinkle-removal is anything but a pipe dream. After years of dating experience, I still haven't worked out all the bugs.

I walked Greg out to the front porch to say goodbye. Max's pumpkin sat where I had left it the night before—waiting for me to take a knife from the kitchen and carve a gap-toothed grin. Waiting for me to return to the task of being a mom.

Greg and I were not a one-night stand. He stuck around. He came to my house for dinner when I had my kids with me. When they went to their father's house, Greg would invite me to his apartment. He'd open his front door at my knock, happy to see me, with upbeat music playing in the background. Before each meal we'd move Greg's roommate's bicycle from where it leaned against the dinner table. Once Greg placed a red rose at my plate. I obsessed over that single rose. I willed the velvet bud to symbolize something grand about Greg's feelings for me; verbal communication wasn't his style. After we ate, we sat on his couch, drank red wine, and nibbled 75 percent dark chocolate before bed.

Greg's bedroom was dark and dank. He kept his window blinds shut at all times, and the sun's warmth did not filter through. Mold grew in his closet. I could smell its rank dampness as it multiplied there.

Greg resisted physical contact with me following sex. He'd become agitated if my body touched his while we slept, and he kept a tally of the number of times I'd stir during the night. Greg never referred to me as his girlfriend, though we dated exclusively for six months. He never told me he loved me, although I told him. That happened only once. He said he didn't feel the same. I never let the "L-word" slip again. February fourteenth came and went without mention. Max asked me to be his Valentine.

Get over it, Rebecca. Don't hold on to your hurts.

February fifteenth: I was running late for my doctor's appointment. I hurried outside to get into my car. A boy from next door came out of his house. It was he, the sweet one of the bunch. Persian? His hair was unruly—dark and curly—already starting to thin on top. *He'll be bald by his 30s,* I thought.

He was dressed casually in plaid shorts, a T-shirt, and sandals. His sandals—tacky multistrapped rubber slip-ons—looked like something an old man would wear. He was a nerd: likely brilliant in class. *And brilliant in bed.*

Stop, Rebecca! Don't go there. He's waaay too young.

Upon seeing me, he raised his hand slightly and offered a shy smile. I opened my driver's door but did not get in. He approached.

"Your car has been gone a lot. I figured you must have a boyfriend."

My face grew warm. (Hot flash?) I kicked at the loose gravel of my driveway.

"Just don't let *him* hear you say that," I joked.

His dark eyes regarded me.

"Well, he's lucky."

My heart raced. (Cardiac arrest?)

"Thank you. You're kind. I'm sorry, but I've forgotten your name."

"Tarek."

I climbed into my car and collapsed into the driver's seat. (A case of the vapors?)

"I'm not feeling well. I'm late. There's somewhere I need to be."

One night Greg and I were alone at my house, sitting on the living room couch. The room was dim—glowing from the light of several candles—the way I like it at night. There was a knock on the door. I got up to answer it. Tarek was there, leaning on the doorjamb, smiling his shy smile. He'd had his hair shaved very short. Tamed. With most of his hair gone, his eyes stood out: two large almonds outlined with a permanent marker of dark lashes. He smelled like beer. It was obvious he'd had a few. He held a CD.

"Hi," Tarek said. "I was walking home from downtown, and I saw your lights. I wanted you to hear Jimi Hendrix play the national anthem at Woodstock."

Greg bent forward to better hear the conversation at the door. He cleared his throat. He bounced his right knee up and down in agitated impatience. "I can't believe this," he complained. I knew Greg wanted me to send him away, but I didn't want to hurt Tarek's feelings.

"Come in, Tarek. Greg and I are just hanging out. All of us can listen to your CD."

Tarek stepped into the living room, and I directed him to the DVD player. Greg stood and stormed out onto the front porch. I tagged after him. Jimi's unmistakable guitar riff followed us into the night.

"Greg, where are you going?"

"I'm going home. If you want to entertain that kid, go ahead. I don't want to waste my time."

Greg had made it clear. He wouldn't waste his time on fat girls or my neighbor. I had a feeling I would be next. Why was he wasting his time on me?

On the other side of the screen door, the neighborhood was quiet—heavy with midnight. Greg jammed his hands into the front pockets of his snug-fitting jeans. I took this as a sign I'd best not approach. My home's porch light illuminated the tips of his curls, transforming them into a silvery halo. Standing there, Greg resembled an angelic totem pole: glorious and wooden. I reached out and gave his shirtsleeve a gentle tug.

"Please, Greg, don't go. I'll ask him to leave."

For a short time, Greg had been married but they'd never had children. I believe this was fortunate. Greg was uncomfortable around my kids—impatient and churlish. On Easter, he hid my young sons' foil-wrapped chocolate eggs so effectively that my children and I continued to find sweet treats in our yard long after Greg's departure from our lives. I've never been certain whether he stowed the candies on too-high branches and within obscure corners out of a sense of fun or mean-spiritedness. My heart gifted Greg the benefit of the doubt. My intuition wasn't so easily duped. If reincarnation exists, Greg was once a lion: a noble beast capable of devouring his offspring.

Greg took me on a trip to Yosemite where we stayed in a quaint hotel, ate soup and sandwiches in front of the fireplace, and went hiking in the spring snow. He volunteered to drive me back to a restaurant

where I'd dropped my glove, and he labored over his camera's tripod so he could take our photo. He allowed me to touch him after sex. I wanted to believe Greg had softened toward me. I hoped our greater intimacy meant he loved me. At a popular vista that featured a regal view of El Capitan, a stranger offered to take our photo. Millions of tourists have such a photo, with their arm casually positioned around a girlfriend, a sister, or a wife. Ours felt contrived. I needed to know the truth about Greg's feelings for me. I zipped my jacket and pulled the fur-lined hood—my protective armor—over my head.

"Do you consider me your girlfriend?"

He cleared his throat. "No, we're just dating."

His dagger-words stabbed me, but I was already on the front line. I charged forward even though I bled.

"After six months, why don't you want to be with me? Why don't you love me?"

"Your life is a roller coaster of kid-induced drama. You and I could never work."

His words had stopped me cold—killed me—but I knew he was right. My children and I were a rollicking package deal. Following my divorce, I had hoped to find a man whose love was big enough to embrace us all. Greg was not the guy for the job. I knew I'd be hard-pressed to find a man who was.

I'd stayed with Greg because I had believed he'd come to love me. I had foolishly invested in wishful waiting with the hope that someday Greg would come around. Greg had stayed with me because he'd wanted companionship. There'd never been anything more to his agenda. We broke up.

Two weeks later, I fell on my rain-slick steps and hurt my back. I called Greg. I told him that I'd been hurt—that I missed him. The next morning, I discovered a fog-dampened note he'd placed under my windshield wiper the night before. The ink had run. The wet weather had transformed Greg's words into a dreamy watercolor that wished me good health. A month later Greg called on Mother's Day to wish me a happy one.

I had other relationships. I had other heartaches. Four years passed. I came across Greg's dating profile on Match.com. I sent him an email and he responded. He invited me to dinner. When I climbed into Greg's truck, I smelled the long-forgotten odor of moldy dampness and Tide. He cleared his throat. Suddenly, I understood Greg's chronic throat clearing in a way I hadn't before. Greg had remained living in the same apartment. The spores, which spread within the recesses of Greg's closet, had continued to invade his clothes, his truck, and his health.

After dinner and a nightcap, Greg suggested we buy a bottle of wine and take it back to my place. I politely declined. Greg wasn't a bad man, but time and a gentler love had separated me from my feelings for him. I could never go back. When he pulled up to my house, I thanked him and got out. I had allowed him to waste too much of my time.

When the Bough Breaks

"**I** LOOOVE YOOOU, REBECCAAA!"

Who was it that loved me?

From outside the bathroom window, I heard the crunch of gravel underfoot. I'd just moved into my house, and there were no window coverings for me to hide behind apart from the shower curtain that encircled my claw-foot tub and veiled the room's tiny window. "I love you too!" I called out from within my enamel tub and vinyl-draped hideaway. What else could I say? "Who goes there?" Overly medieval.

In the house next door a raucous game of beer pong had ensued in the unshuttered living room, transforming it into the lit hollow of a jack-o'-lantern. I assumed the male at my window was a member of the neighboring college clan who'd introduced themselves when I moved in. I couldn't remember any of their names, though it was clear one of them had remembered mine. He howled his drunken sentiment from beneath my window. Dry and fully clothed, I

cowered in my ancient shower, too intimidated to peer out the privy window to discover the identity of my nocturnal Romeo.

I'd never know for certain who it was that called to me that night, but I've got a strong suspicion.

Tarek was an old soul in a young man's body. He was a biology major at Cal Poly, as well as an aspiring musician. Tarek's taste in music ran along the lines of Frank Sinatra, the Moody Blues, and the Beatles. His favorite movie star was Marilyn Monroe. He was rapt over the white leather baby shoes I'd worn in 1959, which dangled from my bedroom doorknob by the laces. One day, Tarek gifted me his high school photo, taken when he was a senior, only three years before. He liked vintage. He liked me. Tarek was my twenty-one-year-old neighbor. I was a forty-nine-year-old cradle robber.

When Tarek first took a shine to me, he would occasionally stop by to visit. One day, he appeared at my screen door as I sat on my living room couch hand-stitching curtains. He had come to deliver a welcome-to-the-neighborhood card signed by him and his roommates, although it was obvious one hand—his—had penned all four signatures. On future occasions, should Tarek appear on my front porch and call my name through the screen door, I invited him in and made him a peanut butter and jam sandwich accompanied by a glass of orange juice.

I am fascinated by how men are typically welcoming of the most humble of culinary offerings. If somebody presented me with a PB&J and a glass of orange juice at four in the afternoon, a mere two hours before dinner, I would politely decline. A man is grateful whenever a woman makes him something to eat, and he'll relish every bite. For some reason, preparing food for a man and watching as he eats it never ceases to endear him to me. When I began to reciprocate Tarek's affections, I upped the quality and complexity of the type of sandwich I served him. The gourmet pesto and melted provolone sandwiches—made with love—may have been the cement that bonded the famished Tarek to me.

The first time Tarek invited me to his room was the night he had dinner with us. My children were excited to have a guest with whom to share their mom's specialty: spaghetti and meatballs. My four young'ins, ages six to fifteen, were welcoming of Tarek. They appeared more comfortable with his presence at our table than he was with theirs. After dinner I readied him with a pale pink Tupperware of leftover spaghetti. Tarek asked if I would come over to watch TV with him after my kids had gone to bed. Later, in his room, Tarek held my face in his hands and silently coaxed me to press my flattened palm to his. I had never been touched with such tender thoughtfulness. His kisses were whispers of smoke that foreshadow a wild fire. Following that night, I no longer viewed Tarek as just a boy.

Frequently, Tarek summoned me from deep slumber by knocking on my bedroom window and crooning, "Rebeccaaa . . ." Then, he retreated to his house to wait. I'd get up, pull on sweatpants and a T-shirt, brush my teeth, and check on my sleeping children. Whenever they stayed at their father's for the night, I exited my house and traipsed across our neighboring dew-laden lawns accompanied by a light heart. The nights my children stayed with me, I went to Tarek carrying a haversack weighted with guilt.

I mounted the rickety wooden stairs that led to Tarek's porch and let myself in through the unlocked door of the house he shared with his buddies. Inside the unlit entry, the aroma of black pepper, stale beer, and unaired linens greeted me. It was an unmistakable guy smell. I inhaled greedily.

Considering its small square footage, Tarek's bedroom held an ample amount of furniture: a twin bed, a full-size upright piano, a desk and office chair, a computer, a floor lamp, a bookshelf, a recliner, a television, one electric and one acoustic guitar, and an array of advanced audio equipment. His walls were decorated with a variety of black-light posters reminiscent of the 1960s. Among his collection of retro art, Tarek had tacked up my photo. I smiled down on his room from my allotted space between Jimi Hendrix and Marilyn Monroe. When I sequestered myself with Tarek in his room, I stepped into a world where I existed only as myself. For a short time, I could pretend I was nobody's harried mother or undermined ex-wife.

Sometimes he wouldn't knock on my window for weeks, and I would let him be. Perhaps Tarek observed my comings and goings as I observed his, yet we each kept our distance. After a time—a few days or several weeks—there'd be a soft rap at my window. He'd call my name so softly that it was difficult to discern if his presence was stationed in reality or within the fading remnants of my dream.

A yearning akin to homesickness compelled me to climb out of bed, ready myself, and follow him. Waves of déjà vu lapped at the shore of my mind as I traversed our front yards, climbed the rickety wooden steps to his porch, and entered Tarek's home. Once inside, I'd stand alone in the darkened entry, close my eyes, and gratefully suck in the pungent testosterone musk. Then I would step through the magic wardrobe that led to Tarek's room: my refuge. For hours we'd lie stretched out on his bed to watch his collection of *Lost* episodes.

There was a time when, every night for two weeks, Tarek came to fetch me. Sometimes I would listen as he practiced his class presentations or played his guitar. Often we would talk about life. Tarek listened to me. Tarek considered the things I said. On each occasion, as the night deepened, I'd leave his room and run across his yard and up the steps of my house to check on my sleeping children. Then I'd run back down the steps, across our yards, and return to Tarek. Breathless. A couple of hours before dawn, Tarek and I would slip under his covers to kiss, love, and curl around one another in his too-small bed.

At six o'clock in the morning, I'd leave Tarek. I would climb beneath my bedcovers where I'd feel more cold and alone than if I had remained in my bed for the night. On occasion I would sleep too long with him. My children would be up and questioning my whereabouts when I arrived home. Once in a while Tarek would knock on my window late at night and I'd invite him to crawl into my bed. Early the next morning, he'd creep past me to exit as I assembled school lunches at my kitchen counter.

It was not easy for me to justify my actions. Excitement and self-reproach staked their claim in neighboring camps.

To me, Tarek was not a sexual toy. But what was I to him? One night he and I lay together on my couch and cried as we listened to John Lennon's "Love"—*Love is you, you and me, love is knowing we can be.* Another time, we slow-danced to velvet-voiced Sinatra—*Two friends drifting apart, two friends, but one broken heart . . .*

A few days later, Tarek showed up unannounced at the paint-your-own-pottery studio where I worked as a shop girl. The bells attached to the door handle signaled I had a customer. My face registered surprise—and then delight—when I saw it was Tarek. He looked dubious. "I've only stopped by to say hello," he said. I watched from the doorway as Tarek began his trek home along Chorro Street. I called out. He stopped and turned. I ran to him and planted a firm kiss on his mouth.

I often wondered what Tarek's roommates thought of us. I was secretly curious if they chided Tarek, or slapped him on the back in a display of congratulatory male bravado. I worried I'd be pegged the neighborhood cougar. I was concerned that my behavior compromised my integrity and my children's well-being. Regardless of our attraction to one another, nothing could rectify the chasm of years that separated Tarek and me. Our relationship was a cruel cosmic joke.

Tarek's mother was not aware of me, although she was aware her eldest son was involved with an older woman. She told Tarek that if she were not happily married, she might entertain the idea of a young lover. Once, I asked Tarek if he'd introduce me to his mother. He said no, because although he knew his mom would like *me*, he was certain she would not approve of *us*. As a protective mother, I understood how Tarek's mom felt about "us."

But fate had its way. One day I found myself standing behind Tarek's mother and his brother in a grocery store checkout line. I was sure the woman was his mom because the boy with her so closely resembled Tarek. When his mother had paid, taken up her groceries, and walked away, I noticed she had left her store discount card on the checkout counter. I ushered the customer behind me to go ahead, and I ran to catch up with Tarek's mother.

"Excuse me, ma'am!"

I called her "ma'am" although she and I were nearly the same age. She was dressed in a brown below-the-knee wool skirt, tailored blouse, cardigan sweater, and sturdy low-heeled pumps. That was how I imagined all levelheaded mothers dressed. Mothers who coupled with age-appropriate partners, and mothers who slept all night, every night, in the same house with their kids. She turned around and faced me.

"You forgot your card at the checkout stand."

"Oh, I guess I did. Thank you."

Without Tarek's assistance, I had managed to meet his mother, all on my own.

One night a month later, I was besieged with an unexpected possessiveness that compelled me to spy. I lifted a corner of my bedroom curtain and witnessed *my* Tarek kissing a girl who stood alongside the beer pong table in his bright jack-o'-lantern living room. She had the long straw-blonde ponytail of a show horse. Her big boobs stood at attention under her bulky hoodie, her head thrown back as she laughed—like a braying donkey—at something Tarek had said. I was ravaged by the green bile of jealousy. Curled protectively like a pill bug, I lay in my bed and cried tortured tears until I fell asleep. I knew Tarek and I were inevitably doomed—it was unreasonable for me to consider any other outcome—yet my heart had dug in its heels, reluctant to face the truth.

Shortly after, I began to date Scott. A native New Yorker, Scott had moved to the Central Coast after he'd secured a job as a physical therapist with a local hospital. He was a handsome man with a full head of lush chestnut-colored hair. His mane resembled Colin Farrell's in the way one rakish lock would fall from his gorgeous crown, down across his forehead, just so. I liked Scott, and I liked that he and I were able to venture out in public and be viewed as an appropriate couple. Scott was a more reasonable choice.

One evening, following dinner in town, Scott walked me home through the quiet of my neighborhood. As we passed a vacant house, I led an unsuspecting Scott inside the walled wraparound porch, pulled him down atop the smooth planks, and wrapped my mouth around his impressive girth. Afterwards, we lay within our shelter and gazed upward at the billowing clouds painted on the sky-blue ceiling of the porch's overhang. I had passed the old craftsman countless times over the years; however, it's doubtful I would have discovered the winsome mural were it not for my detour there with Scott.

We held hands as we approached my house. I knew it would be futile to climb the porch steps to grasp, and then turn, the door's brass knob. After all, the house was locked—my purse and keys, inside. Whenever I walked the short distance into town, I preferred to travel light. I left Scott standing out front as I unlatched the side gate, entered my backyard, and located the spare key I'd hidden under a rusted rabbit doorstop three hours before. I unlocked the back door. I passed through my house and opened the front door for Scott to enter. The man I'd gone to dinner with stood on my porch, yet he'd changed. Deep furrows had transformed Scott's previously unlined brow.

"Rebecca, your neighbor just threw a tantrum on his front porch. He called you a cheater. He said he would never trust you again. What was *that* about?"

Good question. Why would Tarek be upset with me? I hadn't cheated on him. He and I weren't even seeing each other anymore. He had donkey-girl. And I had Colin Farrell.

"Are you sure of what you saw, Scott? Are you sure it was about *me*? He and I are just friends."

"He said your name. It seems he's more attached to you than you think."

My phone rang. It was Tarek. I lifted my left forefinger to signal Scott that I would only be a minute. He sat on the living room couch as I ducked into my bedroom to talk with Tarek.

"Rebecca, who's the guy you're with?"

"He's a friend of mine. He said you threw a fit after we walked up."

"No . . . but we should talk. Come over when he leaves."

I hung up and reentered the living room. I was sorry Scott had been caught in cupid's crossfire, but I was secretly satisfied I'd managed to get under Tarek's skin. I was hopeful he and I still had a chance.

Scott leaned forward and put his forearms on his thighs. He looked up at me. A chestnut lock fell across his forehead, where lines of consternation had given way to defeat. I winced. If social decorum had allowed me an exit, I would've bolted. But I didn't run. My discomfort and I stood smack-dab in the moment of truth.

"What's up, Rebecca? Do you have something going with the kid next door?"

"Well, kinda . . . I don't know. He's not such a kid, by the way. He likes Frank Sinatra."

Scott shook his head. "Tonight I was going to ask you to become exclusive with me, but this development has changed things."

As Scott's words registered, I crossed my arms over my chest. My stance oozed defensiveness. If Scott was suggesting I choose between him and Tarek, I already knew what my answer would be.

"I like you, Scott, but I've liked him longer."

Scott stood and walked toward the door. "This is ridiculous. I'm going to go. You can call me if you change your mind."

I said good-bye to a good man with sexy hair who wanted to be my boyfriend. I watched from my front porch until his truck was out of sight, and then I hurried next door to Tarek. I let myself in the front door and stood in the entryway. The living room was empty, and the ping-pong table, devoid of action. On top of the table sat a small white ball and several red Solo cups: remnants of a happier time. I didn't linger. Hastily, I sucked in the home's man-scent and passed through the magic wardrobe. I heard the Moody Blues on the other side: *Once upon a time, in your wildest dreams . . .* It was uncommonly stormy in Tarek's room. He was angry. Tarek got down to business.

"It's not going to work between us," he said.

"So, you *are* upset with me. You said you weren't."

He ignored me. "I've met a girl who likes me a lot."

"The girl with the ponytail. I know. I saw you together. What are your feelings for her?"

"I'm probably going to go for it."

Tarek had slapped me, right? From across the room I felt the brutal impact of his words.

Though I'd steeled myself against this moment, once it'd come, I was ill-prepared. My world plummeted. I was Alice falling down the rabbit hole. My mind sought something solid to grab ahold of. Panicked by the possibility my photo was gone—*replaced*—I scanned Tarek's bedroom wall. But my picture remained—edges slightly curled—between Marilyn and Jimi. I sighed, grateful for a moment's reprieve. I looked to Tarek. His eyes: dark-lashed almonds. Resting on me. Waiting for me to calm. Patiently waiting for me to focus on him. Sometimes Tarek was older than I.

"Why not me?" I asked.

"You've spoiled me for anybody else, Rebecca. I won't find another woman like you . . . but it can't work between us. You know that."

Did I know that? Yeah, sure I did. But I also knew about the connection Tarek and I shared. I knew how rare it is to find somebody who'll touch you with tenderness and listen to you and dream with you and belly laugh with you. It wasn't his fault. He was still so young. He wouldn't understand about us for years. By that time it would be too late. Too late for us.

As is my way, I rallied in the shadow of defeat: I made a wisecrack.

"Wow, Tarek. Life is crazy. I started the evening with two guys wanting me, but by night's end I have zero men in my corner."

He laughed. We may have had episodes of jealousy and bruised feelings, but there was no bad blood between us.

Tarek's youth hadn't been a deterrent to my heart as it recklessly tumbled and fell in unanticipated love with him. But in the end, I was reminded of what I already knew: the universe is not always benevolent when it comes to affairs of the heart. I went home. Alone. I cried myself to sleep. Again. I'd been pummeled by the punch line of our cruel cosmic joke.

The Cradle Will Fall

FOR A LONG TIME WE'D REGARDED EACH OTHER FROM A DISTANCE. Then, he knocked, on a night I was home alone—without children. When I answered my door, I was surprised to see Tarek standing there. He was weighted with relationship woes and in need of a friend, he said. I'd had hard times, too. I swung the door wide enough for him to enter.

Two years before, as I healed from the heartbreak of Tarek, I messaged Andrew on Plenty Of Fish. Straightaway, he invited me to join him for sushi in Morro Bay. I arranged for a babysitter, slipped into a sundress, donned a pair of flip-flops, and off I went. Perhaps individuals obsessed with the rules of dating etiquette would frown on my eagerness to accept a spontaneous invitation from a man I'd just met, but occasionally, it does one good to eschew the rules and seize the moment. When I arrived at the restaurant Andrew was waiting out front. He shook my hand and introduced himself. Judging from his robust good looks and affable charm, I knew I'd met my match.

It wasn't long before Andrew maneuvered into my life and into my house. He brought along his timid Australian Shepherd, Sonny, whom my children and I adored. I prized the rogue bull-of-a-man that took my life by storm, but mostly, I marveled at his swift and steadfast commitment to *me*.

My new beau could do things that bookish Tarek could not. Andrew knew how to repair my home's *drip, drip, drip* faucets and overtaxed toilet. He replaced rotten redwood siding and poured concrete footings to stabilize the fractured foundation. He rented a backhoe and uprooted my front yard when the drought-plagued lawn withered and died. Perched on top of the yellow Caterpillar like a soldier on a tank, Andrew plowed through overgrown box hedges, unearthed the remnants of an ancient asphalt driveway, and demolished the backyard chain-link fence. Later, he assembled brick planters to corral newly planted freeway daisies and a mimosa sapling with fuzzy pink blossoms. He built an impressive fence from a pile of scrap lumber. He asked me to be his wife.

At Christmastime, Andrew hung icicle lights and tacky tinsel garlands. He impaled a prime rib on the rotisserie, whipped up creamy mashed potatoes, and whipped my booty when I wasn't in bed to please him by nine. His coworkers called him "Hollywood." His smile was a showstopper. But at home, he played the role of Jekyll and Hyde. Over time, I came to love him and fear him in equal measure.

Each night, his muscular arms surrounded me in a protective—*possessive*—embrace while we slept. He was jealous of my neighbor, Tarek. I'd made the mistake of telling Andrew about him. For my moment of impaired judgment, I'd pay a terrible price.

One night, out of the blue, Tarek sent me an unsolicited message while I lay in bed with Andrew. Tarek's *how r u?* text was the pulled safety pin on Andrew's grenade. He exploded. Andrew threatened to knock me silly. And worse. We broke up. Max cried when Sonny jumped into Andrew's truck, and dog and beast drove away.

A month later, Tarek stepped through my doorway. I lit a candle and switched off the living room lights. Faint shadows danced on the pale lavender walls. Cedar and sage perfumed the air. We sat on opposite ends of the couch. Tarek playfully nudged my foot with his. It was good to see him.

Tarek began to talk. Things had not fared well for him and his blonde, ponytailed girlfriend. Apparently, he'd not given her the attention she needed and she went seeking it elsewhere. She'd cheated on him more than once.

I studied Tarek. His looks had matured some—after all, he'd turned twenty-five. As I'd predicted, his hairline had continued to recede, and he kept his hair cut close to the scalp. His bone structure was more defined than when we'd last been in close proximity, but his eyes were the same dark-lashed almonds I remembered. If, by some other strike of fate, we'd been cast as college-age peers instead of May and September, Tarek was convinced I would not have shown him interest. I would've been out of his league, he said, but I disagreed. From the beginning, I'd been drawn to his emotional intelligence and subtle humor. His lights were on. There was always somebody home.

But, as the night progressed, I sensed something vile and drastic had overtaken the sweet introspective young man I'd known. Upon discovering his girlfriend's infidelities, Tarek confessed that he had retaliated with unsavory behavior of his own—with the intention of hurting her. Their bond had become a mess that would be difficult to rectify.

I had always assumed that, if faced with adversity, Tarek would take the high road of a compassionate peacemaker, or simply walk away from a destructive situation with his head held high. I'd been wrong. But he'd been right: maybe I was out of his league after all.

It wasn't until six o'clock the next morning that I extinguished the candle. A thread of smoke trailed upward and dissipated in the scented air. Fully clothed, Tarek and I lay on my bed. Like the peel of a tangerine that encases the fruit, he wrapped his body around mine. When we woke at ten, I made him breakfast: scrambled eggs, toast with jam, and orange juice. Afterwards, I opened my front door on a new day. Tarek and I embraced but did not kiss. He walked down my steps, turned, and raised his hand in farewell.

Go, Dog. Go!

IN HIS ONLINE PHOTOS, HE'D HAD TEETH. All thirty-two of them, lined up in two even rows, just as nature had intended. When we spoke on the phone the first time, Cooper confessed he was minus one upper middle incisor. Prior to our date, he'd wanted me to know what to expect, or in his case, what *not* to expect. As a rule I am partial to teeth. However, as soon as I met Cooper, I became less convinced of the necessity of a complete mouthful.

He stood waiting for me in front of the Monday Club on Monterey Street, where we planned to attend an evening fashion show. I'd never been invited to a fashion show for a first date, or a second date, or on any date, for that matter. I admired the novelty of Cooper's choice. Dressed in denim jeans, a cotton tattersall shirt, and a vintage navy-blue polyester leisure jacket with white topstitching, Cooper cut a fine figure. His missing incisor boosted his boyish appeal. He was unassumingly handsome and gentlemanly. Following our hellos, he extended his arm. Happily, I took it.

As the enthusiastic audience applauded each model on the runway, I sipped a glass of red wine. Cooper downed three. He'd

arrived at the Monday Club via taxicab. Following the show, I drove us to dinner, and then dropped Cooper off at his house. He said he owned a car but didn't drive it. He rode his bicycle to work and everywhere else. *How nice*, I thought. I respect environmentally conscious people.

On date number two, we met at Barnes & Noble. I drove my car and parked in a metered lot that didn't require quarters after six. Cooper rode his bicycle and chained it to a signpost. We sat at a miniature picnic table in the children's section and read aloud from *Go, Dog. Go!*

"'Do you like my hat?'"

"'I do! What a hat! I like it! I like that party hat!'"

I was impressed—charmed, really—that this new man held an appreciation for simple and slightly offbeat activities. For Cooper and me, kid-play was foreplay.

At forty-five, he was one of the youngest members of the Eagles Lodge. I had assumed Cooper enjoyed socializing with vintage people for the same reason he enjoyed donning vintage clothes: they were cool! But when I asked, he made it clear that the elderly folks were not the geriatric hooks that had compelled him to join. Cooper had become a member of the Eagles for the convenience of a bar close to home where he could ride his bike to buy a beer. Or half a dozen.

A week after our first date, I was delighted when Cooper invited me to a dinner party at the home of his married friends, Shelley and Jack. I interpreted it as a positive sign that he wanted to introduce me to his peers. I brought along a loaf of still-warm zucchini bread. Cooper brought a twelve-pack of beer. An appropriate amount of beer for a party of four.

Shelley and Jack resided in a faded chalky-pink mobile home.

Their small front yard sported pink flamingo lawn ornaments, without the lawn. In their later years, my grandpa and his wife had lived in a mobile home, but my parents had always lived in a house. My new grandma would get angry if we called her mobile home a "trailer." My parents would take my sisters and me to our grandparents' to watch the Rose Parade. My step-grandma boiled the frozen vegetables she served us. At home my mother always steamed fresh. I'd never wanted to look down my nose at my grandpa's wife's overcooked green beans and their trailer, but I'm afraid I had.

My definition of a dinner party includes a dining table set with napkins, flatware, water glasses, ceramic plates, and perhaps goblets for wine. Soon after I entered Shelley and Jack's home, I realized that heavy emphasis had been placed on *party* and little on *dinner*. There was no table set in anticipation of good food and lingering conversation. By the time Cooper and I had arrived, our hosts were well into their fourth whiskey sour. Apiece. Shelley assembled a taco casserole. The main ingredient was haste. At seven o'clock, when she pulled it from the oven, Shelley announced, "If anybody wants to eat, dinner is served!"

I stood alone at the kitchen counter to eat my meal and finish my second and final beer of the night. Shelley, Jack, and Cooper drank with no sign of slowing down.

"My dad was a drunken Scotsman," said Jack in his heavy brogue.

"I think I'll mix another," said Shelley.

Cooper didn't say much at all. He was a quiet drunk.

By nine o'clock, Jack had disappeared and Shelley was passed out—slumped over the cold tile counter. She looked uncomfortable. Personally, I think Shelley could have planned better and consumed her final whiskey sour in bed, surrounded by soft pillows and blankets.

It seemed like it was time to go. I suggested we leave. Cooper walked me past the yard flamingos and then stopped short.

"You go ahead. I want to finish my twelve-pack," he said.

"But I'm your ride home."

He glared at me. "Rebecca, I'm staying!"

I've discovered it generally takes seven days to figure out if a new man possesses alarming red-flag qualities. Cooper's week was up. No amount of reading *Go, Dog. Go!* at a child's table would remedy the woes in Cooper's life.

"Sure. No problem—stay."

My words did not match what I really felt. My ire boiled. I wanted to humiliate the man who was rejecting me for less than a twelve-pack of beer.

"Oh, and by the way, how did you lose your front tooth?"

Cooper swayed. "I tripped over a cement parking curb as I was leaving the Eagles Lodge."

"I had guessed it was something like that. Good-bye, Cooper."

I did not like his party hat.

Humps

LARRY, NORM, EUGENE, BERNIE, DICK, LLOYD, AND HAROLD are some of the eligible men I've met online. Probably most women would regard each of these names as an insignificant aspect of the guy who'd asked them out. Not me. I'm a name snob.

When a man initiates online contact, I'm apprehensive until the time he sends an email that concludes with his name. When I saw "Bernie" typed there on my screen, plain as day—in black lettering I could not ignore—I replied. Yet privately, I was disappointed. I just couldn't imagine pillow talk with a man named Bernie. If he'd been a total hunk, maybe his unfortunate moniker would've been palatable. But this Bernie was no hunk. His name had tipped the scales against him, as far as I was concerned. Before we'd had an opportunity to go out, I received an email from Bernie that informed me he'd met a romantic interest. O happy day! Let his new woman vault over the hump of his name.

Then I met Mateo. He was a fellow artist, he displayed genuine interest in me, and he hadn't shied away from making it known that he sought a committed long-term relationship. Granted, Mateo *was* a little slow on the draw. The cogs of our phone exchanges didn't fit like I preferred, but I hoped that once we were positioned face-to-face, Mateo would prove himself a capable conversationalist. Chiefly, I was grateful for his cool name. My fantasies highlighted pillow chats with Mateo. To me, his name was a hump averted. Yet it became clear that whenever I'd bypass one hump, invariably, another would rise up in its place.

Soon after I'd given him my number, Mateo sent a text message— *dO yOu STi11 wanT TO gO OuT?*

Lordy. Mateo had used the number one as a substitute for the letter "L."

Was Mateo's strange text indicative of him being a strange guy? On one hand, Mateo's odd text *was* puzzling, but on the other hand, the man who'd sent it seemed well intentioned. Maybe refusing to date a sweet guy due to the funky nature of his text was pretentious. But truthfully, had Mateo's name been Larry, and if Larry had sent me a text message identical to Mateo's, I would've thrown Larry out on his ear.

On our first date, Mateo showed up thirty minutes late. He'd had to drop his daughter off at her mother's house. I have kids. I understood. We met at a four-star restaurant. I came attired in a black cocktail dress and heels. My curly blonde hair had been subjected to the straightening iron, and it hung glossy and untethered down my back. Mateo wore a bowling shirt, khakis, black Converse, and a knit beanie. When we had been seated at our table, Mateo's beanie remained seated as well—pulled down to cover his eyebrows. He had gorgeous green eyes framed by heavy dark lashes.

Question: Do gorgeous eyes and lashes compensate for a beanie worn at the table?

The waiter brought the wine we'd ordered, and hot bread. I'd yet to determine which side mine was buttered on. I took a stab.

"You wore a beanie in your online photos, too. Do you always wear one?"

"Yeah, I have awful hair." To prove his point, Mateo removed his beanie.

"Your hair doesn't look awful. It just looks like you've been wearing a beanie."

Mateo pulled the beanie down over his head like a cozy condom. His ridiculously long lashes brushed the knit rim. I took a sip of red wine. Then another. I aimed to take the edge off. Mateo chewed spearmint gum as he sipped his pinot noir.

Although our dinner date was not a disaster in any dramatic sense, I just couldn't get over the hump of Mateo's beanie. We didn't see one another until twelve months later when I ran across Mateo's profile again and messaged him hello. He called to ask me out. I said yes—on the condition that he agreed to show up without the beanie.

"Sure, Rebecca. I won't wear my beanie if you promise to wear silk stockings. I love it when women wear sheer stockings."

Hmm.

"I don't own any silk stockings, but I've got black tights."

"No black. I like them nude and shimmery."

Was his a pervy request? I kind of thought so, but I resisted my tendency to overanalyze. I couldn't afford to be picky. By the time I had resurrected Mateo from the tomb of disappointing dates, I'd been marooned for too long on a dateless desert island.

"You drive a hard bargain, Mateo, but I'll see what I can do."

We made plans to get together during the upcoming weekend. In the interim, I shopped online for silk stockings. Things had changed a lot since I'd last purchased them. Back in the day, I'd worn pantyhose with a built-in absorbent cotton crotch packaged in a plastic egg.

I made my online selections: two pair of thigh-high stockings in "Brazil" and "Powder" hues. A six-inch elasticized lace top was designed to keep them from falling down around my ankles. Modern fashion technology is a blooming miracle. I had them shipped express mail.

The second time we went out, Mateo was late by two hours. An hour into his lateness, he texted me a photo of himself wearing a red button-down shirt.

SHOuld i wEaR my ROOmmaTE'S REd SHiRT? my SHiRT iS in THe dRyER.

Sigh. Some things never change. I texted—*Yes! Wear the red shirt already!*

Mateo wore the red shirt. It matched his red truck. The red truck he'd stopped to fill with gas ninety minutes into his lateness. We sat down to dinner at 9:00 p.m. Me, in my lace-topped stockings (I'd worn "Brazil"), and Mateo with his rarely exposed hair, a little scant on top. From the looks of his follicular recession, it was apparent Mateo's beanie had offered excessive coverage. A yarmulke would have done the trick.

The restaurant's ambiance was one of rustic sophistication—very popular in Central California. Patrons were gathered around small wooden tables in twos or fours, and the warm, slightly humid air carried the aroma of sautéed garlic. I was buoyed by the prospect of food and a glass of wine. Mateo chewed spearmint gum. When he spoke, I noticed his top incisors were chipped. During the twelve months since our first date, I had forgotten.

"You seem to enjoy mint gum with your wine," I said. I had forgotten about his gum chewing, too. Middle-aged memory loss is a blessing.

"I never know what to do with my gum. I guess I should excuse myself to the men's room to spit it out."

"That's not necessary. You can spit it into your napkin. I won't tell."

Mateo kept on chewing. In spite of their six-inch elastic top, my stockings were slipping. L'eggs would never have let me down like that.

"I don't drink wine too often because I used to drink too much beer," said Mateo.

"I'm glad you feel you can be open with me."

My encouragement was the magic key that unlocked Pandora's box. Next, I heard about Mateo's lesbian goddaughter and his chronic toenail fungus. By this time he had spit his gum into his napkin, too. The guy had really loosened up.

"You know, a doctor can prescribe an oral medication to clear up your fungus."

"My doctor said an oral medication would overtax my liver on account of my former beer habit."

"I see . . ."

What I really saw was a multitude of humps—a camel train— that I had neither the desire nor the skill to surmount.

Question: Does *not* wearing a beanie at the table compensate for oversharing?

I sighed. "What do you say we order dinner?"

That night I paid for my own supper because Mateo had come up short: on money, a dry shirt, engaging conversation, and the good manners to arrive on time. In the future, maybe I should consider placing less emphasis on a man's given name and more emphasis on his suitability.

maybE i SHOu1d gO OuT wiTH 1aRRy.

A Kiss for Father

AFTER MY MARRIAGE WENT TO HADES, I placed my faith in Match.com: the Promised Land of Internet romance. The site advertised scores of eligible men in my area and age demographic who claimed they sought their "best friend and soul mate." I had hopes my love life would be born again. Then, one day I had an epiphany. Despite what they preached, not all men who subscribed to dating sites were righteous, nor did they all seek eternal love—at least not with me.

Soon after I met Nathan on Match.com, it became clear: I was not his answer to prayer. In a three-week period, Nathan had called only twice. Most often he would text. A grown man who is truly motivated to woo a woman knows better than to rely on the ambivalence of a text to do the job. When Nathan texted to invite me to six o'clock Sunday Mass at the Old Mission, I was surprised, but unimpressed. Had he sent me an old-fashioned invitation by mail? I would have married him.

"Good heavens and what the hell!" I'd proclaimed to my four walls. "I may as well go."

I'm not Catholic. I was raised up in the faith of the Lutheran Church Missouri Synod, kissing cousins of the Catholic Church. Religiously, every Sunday, our handsome pastor donned a colorful stole in accordance with the church season. And he always wore a long white robe—even after Labor Day. In the years leading up to my divorce I'd distanced myself from organized religion. I had begun to piece together my own spiritual identity instead of allowing an ordained minister to dictate my beliefs about God.

Yet I decided to attend Mass as a way to convene with text-loving Nathan. Lord knows, I had zero compulsion to sit in the shadow of an outdated version of God Almighty. I was convinced that nothing enlightening could occur in a conventional Catholic service. Since I knew God loved me but Nathan didn't, I brought along my ten-year-old son, Max.

We met Nathan outside the mission chapel at a few minutes before six. From a distance, Max and I had easily spotted Nathan as he approached. He was a big man, at least six-three, muscular, and well over two hundred pounds. We said our introductory hellos at the upper fountain—the one laden with thick moss—and entered the sanctuary through ancient wooden doors. Nathan made the sign of the cross: his hand to forehead, chest, left shoulder, and then right. We seated ourselves in a pew as the service began. The traditional Catholic liturgy was similar to what I'd recited in the Lutheran Church, but kneeling is something Lutherans don't do. Max and I followed Nathan's cues.

At a priest's instruction, Nathan, Max, and I held hands for a moment's meditation. I'd felt close to tears when Nathan took my left hand in his huge one and I reached to grasp Max's small moist paw in my right. As the reverent crowd bowed their heads, I gazed around at the families whose hands connected them—as if family unity were the most obtainable thing in the world. I was envious. I missed the comfort and togetherness of being part of a nuclear family. For the hour's time Mass had allotted me, I decided to make believe that Nathan, Max, and I were a family too. Following a hymn, Max turned to me and said, "Mom, I'm having so much fun!"

When it came time for the parishioners to step forward for Holy Communion, I told Nathan that Max and I would pass. Although I had been confirmed in the Lutheran Church when I was a teen, I was no longer clear on how I regarded the sacrament of Communion. Nathan encouraged Max and me to stand in a separate line to receive a priest's blessing, without the wafer and wine of Holy Communion.

With Max at my side, we exited our pew and waited on the timeworn floor that had supported a multitude of churchgoers since 1772 when Father Serra had founded the mission. I looked around at the smooth adobe walls, exposed wooden beams, and gilded statues. Just by being in attendance, I had become part of the rich history of this cool dim place that carried the heavy-aired scent of a root cellar. The line shortened and my turn had come. I stood face-to-face with a robed priest.

"Hi, Father. I'm here for a blessing, but I don't know what I'm supposed to do."

"Well," said the elderly priest, "why don't you give *me* a blessing?"

Moments before I hadn't known what to do, but suddenly I had no doubt. I placed my hands on either side of the priest's kindly face and tilted his bald head toward me. I placed my lips on his smooth dome and kissed him, leaving glossy sparkles where my mouth had been. "Bless you, Father," I said.

At the end of the service, the priest rose to address his congregation. A small area high on his forehead glistened beneath the altar lights.

He said, "This evening a woman came forward to receive a blessing from me, but it was I who was blessed. Thank you. Go in peace."

Absolutely. I went in peace. Max appeared peaceful as well. As for Nathan, if he left Mass with a parcel of peace, it never translated to him asking me out again. But that's not to say he didn't text. About every two weeks I'd receive an incoming text from Nathan—

You been to Mass lately?

No, I think the other priests may be mad at me!

Yeah, you're probably right! Your sparkles have incited the clergy to mutiny.

Did I embarrass you when I kissed the priest?

No. I was jealous!

Then, fourteen days later . . .

Is the weather hot enough for you?

It's a scorcher for November! I had to take my sundresses out of storage.

Are they short?

After a while, I surmised that Nathan would never ask me out. Perhaps he texted only to check if I was still interested, or maybe I supplied him an ego boost when he was feeling low. He would shoot me a text message, and I would respond. To Nathan, our exchange was a low-effort, low-risk endeavor that supplied him with the buzz of an incoming text. It is not unusual for men to communicate with women solely in this fashion. I suppose they do it because some women will accept it as acceptable. After two months of Nathan's aimless messages, I texted him—

I think you're a swell guy but I'm not seeking a text buddy.

I never heard from ole Nathan again.

❧

The moral of the story? If you should happen to attend a traditional Catholic Mass with a hunky guy as your date, never assume it will be him you'll kiss. God does indeed work in mysterious ways.

Go in peace.

Handicapped Heart

"GIMPY" WAS THE WORD MY MOTHER USED to describe an individual with short leg syndrome. That was back in the 1970s when "cripple" was also acceptable, as was "handicapped," and "invalid." These terms have always felt foreign—bitter—on my tongue. I've avoided them. In the last forty years, society has steered toward more compassionate—politically correct—terminology. Nowadays, "disabled person" is the right thing to say. "Disabled person" melts in my mouth.

Subsequent to my divorce, I went on a date with a disabled person.

Todd arrived at Steamers before me—*waaay* before me. I should've realized Todd would be early for our first date. During our initial phone conversation, he had informed me that his condition compelled him to be a perpetual early bird. Careening into a parking space as the clock struck the appointed hour, and then making a beeline for the restaurant's front door, was a luxury not afforded Todd.

On the flip side, robust health and good fortune had gifted me the slovenly privilege of "no time to spare." I'm habitually late. Usually,

I squeeze in *one* more chore before leaving the house for a dentist appointment or to pick up my kids after school. Heaven knows there's always a plant to water, an overdue email to send, a kitchen counter to wipe, or a spider to be transported outside on a tissue. For Todd, life circumstances required he show up to appointments or events well in advance. Once he was situated, he waited. Knowing this, I should've made a greater effort to be on time.

Five o'clock traffic from San Luis Obispo to Pismo Beach was heavier than I had expected. The dual lanes of slow-moving cars conjured memories of nightmares in which I ran but got nowhere. I almost missed the Price Street off-ramp. At the last minute I cut in front of a Ford Escort, exited the freeway, and turned right onto Shell Beach Road. The afternoon had waned, and dusk descended like a shade drawn over a bright windowpane. The setting sun was a persimmon-hued fireball that blazed upon the horizon, and then extinguished itself in the icy Pacific. If I hadn't had somewhere to be, I would've savored the view. In lieu of that, I sweated.

I lowered my driver's window to get some air. But not *too* much air. Too much air would ruin my hair. I opened my window a crack to allow a whisper of breeze to enter—just breeze enough to keep me from melting into a syrupy puddle on top of my bucket seat. I pulled over on the sand-dusted strip that borders the road and turned off my car's engine, but left the key in place. The vehicles on the adjacent 101 southbound made a rhythmic *whoosh-pause-whoosh* as they passed. I dialed Todd. He picked up on the second ring.

"Hello?"

"Hi, it's Rebecca. Obviously I'm late. I'm having trouble pinpointing Steamers."

"How close do you think you are?"

"If we were playing a game of hot and cold, I'd be very warm."

Indeed, I *was* very warm. *To hell with my hair!*

Utilizing my left forefinger, I applied steady pressure to the button that controlled the driver's automatic window. I watched as the tinted sheet of glass descended, and then disappeared, inside the door panel. A frigid gust—*a breath of fresh air*—filled my car's interior. I inhaled the briny perfume, switched on the interior light, and peeked at my face in the rearview mirror. Mascara intact. Lipstick luscious. But my hair was hopeless. My carefully flat-ironed locks had returned to their wild state. I shivered. Goosebumps appeared on my bare arms and legs.

"You're probably headed in the wrong direction," said Todd. "Turn around. Be on the lookout for a sign that reads Steamers. I'm waiting in the lounge."

The musicality of Todd's accent was pure Minnesotan. I relaxed a little—smiled. As a rule, I enjoy touching base with a man immediately before our first meet up. A brief phone chat is an icebreaker. It helps alleviate pre-date jitters.

A life-size fiberglass swordfish hung on the section of wall above the restaurant's exterior front doors. Had this not been the beach, but rather, a mountain location, I supposed a taxidermy elk or moose head—maybe a towering grizzly—would've been showcased on the premises instead. I entered the foyer and spotted Todd: a handsome man in a wheelchair positioned at a table for two. Although I'd prepared myself, the sight of Todd's chair was a shock. An instinctual impulse—fight or flight—coursed through me. I battled the urge to turn and bolt. But I didn't run. I stood in the entry and drank up the barroom scent: fried calamari, polished wood, and spicy aftershave, with a twist of freshly squeezed lime.

I walked over to Todd and introduced myself. He looked up and smiled. Yet, unlike any date before or since, Todd did not rise from his chair to wrap me in a hearty hug, nor did he extend his hand in a cordial how-do-you-do. I'd already absorbed the reality of Todd's wheelchair, but now, standing before him, I stole a look at his hands. At rest in his lap, Todd's hands were partially concealed in the fingerless gloves of a competitive cyclist. *To protect his skin as he maneuvers his chair*, I thought. All ten digits curled inward—fingertips touching palms—forming two loose fists.

I sat across from Todd. A waitress approached. I ordered chardonnay; Todd, a martini. As we waited for our drinks, Todd shared a tale from his Midwestern upbringing and spoke of his nine-to-five—a job that required he wake at four in the morning to shower, dress, and leave his house by eight. Our waitress returned. She placed two small square napkins on our small square table. Faint rings of moisture appeared on each napkin as she centered our drinks. I took a sip of wine. Todd told me about the long-ago motorcycle accident that had left him a paraplegic with limited use of his hands.

My glass was nearly empty when Todd finally situated both curled hands around the narrow stem of his martini glass. He raised it to his lips and drank. Suddenly, the fluted glass slipped from Todd's precarious grasp and fell. It struck the tabletop. The resulting *ping* reverberated in the bell tower of my mind.

Clear liquid flowed across the table: a flash flood of vermouth and gin. A pimento-stuffed olive rolled across the sleek wood surface and stopped at the base of my wine glass. Under different circumstances, the renegade garnish would've provoked my ebullient laughter, but on this occasion it had the opposite effect. My face froze in mortified disbelief. Not knowing what else to do, I sprang from my seat, jogged to the elegant stretch of bar, and requested a damp towel. The bartender tossed me a dingy cotton rag—frayed on one edge—that dutifully absorbed the capsized cocktail. Todd apologized. I assured him all was well. Neither of us believed it.

The extent of Todd's physical challenges and the toppled martini had unnerved me. I was relieved we'd planned to meet for only a drink. I couldn't have handled dinner.

My date paid the bill and we prepared to leave. To exit, I stepped outside, held the front door wide open, and waited while Todd jockeyed his wheelchair through. Just before the door closed on the dusky ambiance, I spotted an acquaintance and his wife sitting at a nearby table. I hoped they hadn't seen me.

A cold wind whipped through the building's outer corridor and wreaked additional havoc on my hair. *I probably look like tumbleweed,* I thought. I faced Todd, leaned down, took ahold of his right hand, and gave it a squeeze. "I'm freezing! Thank you for the drink! Have a great evening!"

I disappeared into the parking lot and located my car. Noble compassion—my belief that I was a decent human being—had escorted me to Steamers, but it was shame and guilt that drove me home. Later that evening, I composed an email to Todd—*Thanks again for the drink. I enjoyed our time but I don't think I'm the best match for you. Well wishes on your search for love. ~Rebecca*

I don't remember if Todd replied.

When I'd first spotted Todd on Match.com it hadn't registered as significant that all of his photos were shot from the waist up. I had simply determined Todd attractive and "normal" (free of obvious psychopathic traits), so I messaged him. In his return email, Todd disclosed his wheelchair dependency. Up until the time I'd met him, my dating criteria included "able-bodied" men. Period. After Todd's belated announcement, I was confused. Should I proceed with this man? I decided it was time for a dose of serious soul searching. My thirteen-year-old daughter, Nelly, helped out.

"Mom, you've always taught us kids that it's the person on the inside that counts. I think the only reason you don't want to date this guy is because he's in a wheelchair. That seems wrong."

Nelly was right of course—she usually is. But, although I'd followed her urging and went out with Todd, in the end, I couldn't overlook his disability. My discomfort and unpreparedness—*my fear*—wouldn't allow me to discover the man Todd was inside.

In the years since my date with Todd, I've become intrigued with able-bodied individuals who've paired with disabled partners. I try to imagine what their day-to-day is like. I wonder if they're content being together, and if, and how, they have sex. I've come to realize these couples share something special: a capacity for empathy and love that's farther-reaching than my own.

If ever I were to become dependent on a wheelchair, I'd hope men would continue to view me as worthy of their love, yet, when Match.com introduced me to Todd, I couldn't envision him as my romantic partner. I've wrestled with my hypocrisy, but it persists. When I reflect on the way I behaved with Todd, I feel like I've been stabbed in the heart. Acknowledging my cowardice, arrogance, and desire for the status quo brings me a lot of pain. Whereas Todd could not alter his circumstances, I believe I've the capacity to change, although truthfully, not the fortitude. I'm an able-bodied woman with a handicapped heart.

Walkin' Tall on the Road to Nowhere

H E LOOKED LIKE A WINNER. He *was* a winner. For years, Kevin had been the golden boy at the real estate brokerage firm where he was employed. He brought home the bacon by the truckload. His features were stereotypically All-American. Kevin resembled the actor Parker Stevenson from the Hardy Boys Mystery Series of the 1970s: tall, athletic, and amiable, with close-set blue eyes and hair the color of ripe wheat. I supposed most women found him attractive, and I sincerely wanted to be numbered among them. I realized it would be foolish to pass him by. In the end, I could not muster romantic feelings toward Kevin for reasons that may have appeared supercilious, but they'd spoken volumes to me.

Following a brief online exchange and a couple of phone conversations, I met Kevin for wine in downtown San Luis Obispo. Things had gone well enough, and he had asked me out again. The next week, I drove the few miles north to Paso Robles to visit Kevin at his newly remodeled ranch-style home situated on several oak-studded acres.

I rang the bell and Kevin opened his front door. He smiled. I'm a sucker for a man's bright smile, but although Kevin had beautiful teeth and practiced excellent dental hygiene, something was off. His grin was a lackluster display of teeth and gums and lips stretched tight. His mouth smiled, but his face—his eyes—did not. What a disappointment. What a waste of wonderful teeth.

Kevin was dressed in sand-colored pleated slacks and a blue cotton dress shirt. Pleated slacks and dress shirts are somewhat foreign to me; most of the men in my life wear Levis and T-shirts. When Kevin greeted me in his stocking feet, I immediately understood.

"Is yours a shoe-free home?" I asked.

I looked down to consider my footwear. They were black suede ankle boots with four-inch heels and tassels on the zippers. There was a slight sheen on each toe where the nap had worn thin.

"I usually remove my shoes because this is a rural area. So much dirt!"

"I'd like to keep mine on if you don't mind."

The physical disparity between six-foot-one Kevin and myself was too great. I needed all the height I could get. I wanted to enter Kevin's home walkin' tall.

The scent of fresh paint and recently laid carpet accosted me as I stepped into the entry. Though I'd been granted permission to wear my boots inside, I remained self-conscious when I stepped onto Kevin's spotless carpet. I was self-conscious when I used the sink in the hall bathroom, too. I worried Kevin would notice if I accidentally left water droplets on the granite countertop. After I washed my hands and turned off the vanity's faucet, I wiped the entire countertop with a wad of toilet paper and flushed it along with my pee.

His home's floor plan was open and airy. Every square inch

was fastidiously maintained. Monolithic stone countertops were installed everywhere countertops were called for: the kitchen, the laundry room, and each of the three bathrooms. Kevin's residence housed a Rocky Mountains' worth of granite. An expansive grid of sand-colored grout outlined the terra-cotta tiles that paved the entry, kitchen, laundry room, and bathroom floors. Low-pile carpet the color of Kevin's pleated slacks covered everything else. Kevin was in the process of decorating. He'd purchased a huge leather sectional in a shade identical to his slacks, his carpet, his walls, and his grout. Kevin's ocean liner of a couch was positioned in front of a huge wall-mounted flat-screen TV. It was bold and black. When it came to couches and TVs, Kevin meant business.

Kevin's living room space was undecorated except for two Thomas Kinkades hung on adjacent walls. I stood before each. The first painting depicted a mist-shrouded churchyard, steepled chapel, and tiny arched bridge. A warm light glowed from inside the white chapel. The second painting was of a row of Victorian-style cottages with an American flag waving from a front porch. Kevin switched on two small lights mounted to the rococo-styled frames. He stood beside me to study one painting, and then the other. Kevin's stance was equally weighted with his feet about twelve inches apart. He raised his right index finger and thumb to his chin; his left palm supported his bent elbow. Kevin's demeanor told a story: he was thoughtfully inspired.

"Do you notice how the shimmering paint makes the scene come alive?"

"Yes, Kevin. Whether people appreciate his work or not, one thing is certain, Thomas Kinkade found a niche that made him rich!" It was the kindest comment I could conjure. I'd had to dig deep.

"Did you know he's called the painter of light?"

"Yes, little twinkly lights. His paintings remind me of Santa's Village."

Kevin was nice. He still liked me though I'd compared Tom K. to Saint Nick.

"Are you ready to go to dinner?" Kevin asked.

"What a great suggestion! I'm starved!" I *was* starved—for air that smelled like sautéed garlic and fresh bread, not new carpet and fresh paint.

Once we'd been seated in a booth at his favorite restaurant, Kevin set his menu aside.

"I don't need to look at the menu. I always order the same thing—meatloaf. It's delicious."

"Well, well." I sounded like my mother did when she was less than pleased.

Undoubtedly, Kevin was not ranked among the most adventurous of eaters. I opened my menu to survey my options. I noticed the meatloaf was the least expensive entrée.

If it had been *I* who was taking a new love interest to a restaurant I frequented, I would study the menu and *pretend* to vacillate between the petite sirloin smothered in portobello mushroom sauce accompanied by grilled asparagus, *or* the pesto-basted chicken breast with rosemary red potatoes. Even if I knew full well I'd resort to ordering my usual, I would take a few moments to ponder the menu so I'd appear avant-garde in the eyes of my date. After an appropriate amount of time had passed, I'd close my menu, look to my hot date, and say, "Naww, tonight I want something simple. I think I'll order the meatloaf. But, *pleeease* hot-date-that-I-hope-to-lock-lips-with-later-on, order *anything* you want." That's how *I* would conduct myself if I were dining with a date I strived to woo.

As it was, Kevin's meatloaf had put me in a pickle. It would be downright nervy of me to order something more expensive—for example, the capellini with sautéed shrimp in creamy garlic sauce—if Kevin chose the budget-minded meatloaf. When the waitress approached our table, I couldn't rally the courage to go for the shrimp. I ordered the meatloaf. I like meatloaf. Although not as much as I like sautéed shrimp in creamy garlic sauce served over capellini. Al dente.

But Kevin had been right. The meatloaf was delicious. I ate every bite.

The sun had set by the time Kevin drove his white Chevy Silverado into the driveway.

"Do you need to go home, or would you like to stay and have wine on the patio?"

I hadn't begun to like Kevin yet, at least not in the romantic sense, so I figured I should allow myself more time. Perhaps a glass of wine would help to resurrect my deadened libido.

"Sure, I can stay for a while. It's such a pretty night. A glass of wine on the patio would be lovely."

Kevin took a bottle of chardonnay from his refrigerator. I brightened. Maybe this wouldn't be so bad. He turned to me, and there it was again: his counterfeit grin.

"Would you mind if I poured your wine into a plastic cup? I don't want to risk broken glass on the patio."

"No, I don't mind."

I lied. Deep in my heart, I do mind Dixie.

Mature oak trees canopied Kevin's patio, yet no leaves had fallen onto his pavers. This is an impossibility, as anybody who has oak trees near their patio will tell you. Not so at Kevin's house. His entire pad was a no-muss zone. Kevin built a small fire, and we sat in low-seat beach chairs. The stars had come out. I sipped my chardonnay. I listened to the distant howl of coyotes.

"Rebecca, does the howling of coyotes scare you?"

"No. I think a coyote's howl is hauntingly beautiful."

"Well, I'm afraid of them. When I hear them, I lock all of my windows and doors."

"What do you think they'll do?"

"Coyotes just frighten me, that's all."

I'd tried my darnedest to kindle a spark of sexual desire for the guy, but his girly-man comments doused my libido. The situation was hopeless.

"In rare cases a coyote may go after a child or a small dog, but you fall into neither of those categories, Kevin. The odds are you'll be fine."

Perhaps for the sake of his coyote-loving guest, Kevin remained on his patio instead of barricading himself behind locked doors. He moved his chair closer to mine.

"Do you like to kiss?"

"Yes, I do," I said.

"Then maybe it's just *me* you don't want to kiss."

I said nothing. He was right about more than the meatloaf.

My older children resided with their father, so I couldn't use them as an excuse why I needed to hit the road. But eleven-year-old Max still lived at home. Although I'd left him with a babysitter, I feigned something about my son expecting me. I rose from my beach chair and accidentally kicked over my cup. Wine splashed onto Kevin's leaf-free, glass-free patio. "Thank goodness for Dixie!" I said.

I took ahold of either side of my skirt, bowed my head slightly, and curtsied. And then, I drove away from Kevin's immaculate kingdom. On the way home, traveling inside the box of my car wrapped in midnight, I got lost. But I didn't care. It felt great to be on the road to nowhere.

Date with Serendipity

I'D HAD IT. I'd grown weary of the unreliability of dating sites to procure me viable male options. I had become frustrated with the customary cyber-match routine of initial contact, emails exchanged, phone calls received, and plans to meet. Then there'd be the prep of hair, clothes, and makeup—not to mention childcare arrangements. All for a date where more times than not, chemistry and compatibility were nil. When I first began to date online, I imagined it would prove productive. The reality was: the majority of my experiences were downright discouraging. I'd arrive for a first date, smile, say hello, and shake his hand—as if contented with our match—but often, I fought the impulse to break and run. Sometimes my favorite part of the date was when I drove away. I was grateful for my car. My car was my speedy getaway.

Social outings with my girlfriends had proved an equally ineffective way to meet eligible men. The majority of my gal pals had been hitched for years, thus unavailable for a frolic in the land of unbridled testosterone. When I'd hang with the marrieds, we ladies tended to follow our habitual shtick. We would visit a quiet café where we'd hunker down at a secluded table to submerge ourselves in wine, appetizers, and meaningful girl-talk. (Oxymoron?) Occasionally, we'd visit a pub. I'd sit on a barstool sipping my drink and make sly appraisals of men from across the room. Action seldom ensued. It's a rare maverick that'll penetrate a fortress of women. I was fed up with waiting for a man to make his move online or off. It was time I put myself out there, without the Internet, or my safety net of one or more female friends.

One Saturday afternoon my teenage daughter transformed my long curly hair into a sleek gold mane reminiscent of Malibu Barbie. At my daughter's masterful hand, I was brushed with bronzer and blush, thick mascara, and smoky eye shadow. I slipped into a black minidress. Next, I pulled on my black suede ankle boots with tassels on the zippers. Their four-inch heels elongated my toned legs. I was glad I'd kept up my daily runs on Cerro San Luis. I painted my lips with sparkling pink gloss and walked through a cloud of *Angel* perfume sprayed into the air. My mirror on the wall said, "Not bad!" With that assurance, I headed into downtown San Luis Obispo.

Anybody familiar with "SLO-town" will tell you it is aptly named. People live in San Luis Obispo for predominantly two reasons. Either they are a college student attending Cal Poly State University, or they're an individual who values the outgoing camaraderie and easygoing lifestyle of the small town. Oprah has dubbed San Luis Obispo the happiest city in America. She was definitely on to something. A woman out in San Luis Obispo by herself on a Saturday night has no reason for alarm. In the sixteen years I called this sector of Central Coast my home, I never felt at risk when I ventured out among its population of very contented people.

I met a girlfriend downtown for a happy hour glass of wine. The slight chardonnay buzz helped bolster my resolve to step out solo. I didn't have an agenda for approaching men in bars because I'd never done it before. I decided to make up my game plan as I went along. I flew by the spaghetti straps of my little black dress.

I said *adios* to my friend and strolled the sidewalk, stopping in front of pubs that looked interesting. I passed several bars before I spotted one that seemed conducive to a bit of impromptu socializing. A group of men in their thirties sat at an impressive mahogany bar situated just inside the open door. A man looked in my direction and smiled. I accepted his pleasant countenance as my green light. I stepped in. I approached a stool at the end of the bar. It looked like a good place to "belly up," so I did.

"Hi," I said to the dude with the friendly face. "Is this stool taken?"

He looked mildly startled. "No, it's all yours."

I climbed up. I'm only an inch over five feet. I would have benefited from a step stool to climb on top of my barstool.

"Thanks for being so nice. I'm out on my own to meet single men, and I'm not too sure what I'm doing. This is my first stop. I'm a little nervous." I ordered a glass of wine.

"Well, I admire you. A lady going out by herself is gutsy."

"Do you live in San Luis?" I asked.

"No, I'm from San Francisco. Me and a bunch of my friends are here for the weekend. We're planning to do some wine tasting and go to the beach. My girlfriend is shopping for a bikini."

Ah-ha! The pesky girlfriend! It was predictable that she'd be hiding in the shadows, ready to ruin everything. A young woman approached and nuzzled her guy. She pulled a colorful mass of strings and tiny swatches of fabric from her shopping bag. The aforementioned bikini, I presumed.

"Well, nice to meet you," I said as I hopped down from my barstool. Not knowing what awaited me, I felt like I was free-falling. Back on the sidewalk, I discovered the challenge of distance walking in high-heeled boots. I realized I couldn't walk efficiently unless I took lengthy strides. In other words, I had to "strut my stuff" to make any progress whatsoever. At first I felt self-conscious about my haughty gait—normally I was a running shoes or flip-flops kind of gal—but I resolved to relax, drop all pretense of shyness, and go for it. I strutted. And it felt really good—actually, empowering. As I walked (strutted) along the sidewalk, a man came from behind, passed me, took several additional steps, and then turned around.

"You're gorgeous. Can I buy you a drink?"

I guessed him at about fifty: compact body, dark hair, and average-Joe face. He wore a St. Louis Cardinals varsity jacket. It's mystifying why men choose to wear team jackets of this type once they've graduated from high school sports. I wasn't particularly attracted to the man, yet there I was, out by myself, strutting through town in pursuit of adventure. *And* he'd said I was gorgeous, so I said yes. We entered a nearby restaurant and sat at a small table adjacent to the bar. The man bought me a glass of wine and a dinner of steamed veggies and hummus. He had insisted. Wouldn't take no for an answer. I dipped a julienned carrot into my hummus: a creamy beige jacket encasing vibrant orange.

"I'm in the midst of an adventure," I said.

He stared at me with infatuated goo-goo eyes. "What do you mean by that?"

Before I could reply, the man picked up his phone to retrieve a text message. Then he answered an incoming call. I waited until he'd tied up his business.

"I'm out on the town by myself, and I'm meeting people I never would have if I'd been out with my girlfriends. I have absolutely no idea what may happen next."

"Wow, that's cool, I guess. I apologize for the interruptions. If we were on a real date, I wouldn't be on my phone. Can I see you again?" His phone rang.

"No, thank you. I've appreciated the meal, though."

I moseyed past a pub opened to the street, where three men sat at a table intended for four. I doubled back. I approached their table and asked if they objected to me joining them. I love this about men: hands down and without exception they'll accommodate a lady. Undoubtedly, I'd surprised them when I appeared out of nowhere to solicit their company, yet they invited me to sit in the vacant chair.

The guys were construction workers from out of town. One of them was married, one recently divorced, and the third man aimed to break free of the old ball and chain. He said he was currently involved in an affair with a married woman. I raised an eyebrow at my new friend's confession. One can certainly learn a lot about a stranger by strutting into a tavern and plopping down in an empty chair. The guys drank beer and ate pizza. The divorced member of the trio paid for my glass of wine. I told them I was on the town by myself. I told them I was out to hone my dating confidence by approaching men. All three agreed it was a courageous thing for me to do.

"Would you mind standing on your chair so we can get a better look at you?" asked the happily married man. His request made me doubt the happiness of his wife.

"No, I won't do that. I'm not drunk enough."

They got a kick out of that. They admired my pluck.

When I had finished my wine, I stood—on the floor, not on my chair—and said my good-byes.

"Can I follow you down the street?" said the unfaithful husband.

Apparently, cheating on his wife wasn't enough. He was itching to cheat on his married girlfriend too.

"No, you can't follow me! Like I told you, I'm on an independent adventure. How am I supposed to be on an independent adventure if you follow me down the street?"

On the sidewalk again, I encountered two cute Australians in conversation (that's how I knew they were Australians).

"Hey guys, I'm out by myself. Where are you headed?"

"We're goin' over to Frog & Peach Pub. We'll meet you there."

Men were falling into my lap. I was the queen of Higuera Street. I just couldn't lose.

I strutted into the dimly lit Frog & Peach and made a beeline for the bathroom. When I returned from the loo (what I supposed native Australians would call it), I surveyed the bar. The two cute Australians were nowhere to be seen. They had ditched me! Suddenly, they weren't so cute anymore.

Disappointment and humiliation were lumps of raw dough in my gut. I chastised my ego for being so . . . egotistical! Then I stopped. I regained my composure. *So what* if I'd been riding tall on my high horse! And *so what* if I'd been stood up by two down-unders! I reminded myself that the night wasn't about my expectations of what *should* happen. The night was about me embracing whatever *did* happen.

I spotted a handsome guy sitting by himself at the end of the bar. I walked over.

"Hi, my name's Rebecca. I've been stood up by two Australians. Do you mind if I sit with you?"

"No, I don't mind at all. I'm Sam. What are you drinking?"

I sipped my wine and Sam sipped his beer. We pivoted on our stools to face one another. Our knees touched. Sam told me he was married and had several young children. His wife had decided she didn't love him anymore. She was having an affair with an older man, so Sam had recently filed for divorce. My town was a den of iniquity. There was no avoiding the epidemic of hanky-panky that ran amuck.

I sensed Sam required more comfort than multiple beers could afford him. "I'm sorry to hear your sad tale about your wife. The road to romantic bliss is sometimes a dead end, isn't it?"

Sam was forlorn and sweet and vulnerable. I imagined he needed me, and for the moment, perhaps he did. From atop my stool, I leaned toward Sam. Utilizing an elastic band I pulled from my purse, I swept his wavy shoulder-length hair into a David Beckham–style ponytail. Instead of returning to the loo to reapply, I handed Sam my wand of lip gloss and he painted my lips in pink sparkles. We kissed. Sparkles clung to Sam's five-o'clock shadow and twinkled there like minute stars. We exchanged business cards.

I got up to leave, even though what I wanted was to stay with Sam. I got up to leave because I felt myself being pulled by my attraction to him and it scared me. I wanted to stay because I hadn't felt that pull for quite some time. I hadn't expected Sam to happen, but once he had, I knew it would go no further. At least not that night.

"Well, Sam, I think I have one more barhop in me before I go home. Thank you for the wine."

"Maybe you should call it good and end your adventure with me."

I was disarmed by this man's unassuming charm.

"Okay, my adventure ends with you."

I locked my arm in his and we set out in search of my car. I drove Sam to his friend's noodle shop where he planned to spend the night in the loft above the restaurant. We kissed good-bye through

the open window of my car. Early-morning fog had descended on Palm Street and swathed Sam in a cloud of fine mist. I stuck my left arm out of my window to wave farewell. Then, I drove myself home.

I saw Sam once after that. One week later he came by my house at two o'clock in the morning. As the pub had closed, he called me. He assured me he would run the several blocks from downtown to my house. After Sam called, I switched on my porch light and stood in the fog to wait. It wasn't long before tiny beads of moisture adhered to my arm hair. I supposed I resembled a spider's web that shimmered with morning dew. Sam ran up, and stopped in front of me. I smiled. Mist clung to his eyelashes and five-o'clock shadow. He was a dew-spangled spider's web too.

"It's good to see you," I said. For the past seven days, I'd been expecting him.

We went inside my house. Warm. Quiet. My son was asleep. We sat together on my living room couch. The only light came from a candle I had lit before I'd gone outside to wait. I told Sam his damp wool sweater smelled like dog.

"I can take it off if you'd like."

"Nooo, you'd better leave it on. It's safer that way."

In the moment, I saw Sam and myself as we were. *Me*: a petite middle-aged woman, dressed in a black tank top and pink pajama bottoms patterned with gray snowflakes, long hair mussed from sleep. A barefooted woman who often bared her heart too soon— before hers had been satiated. *He*: a winsome, sad-eyed man, who wanted badly to please, yet had somehow failed to please his wife. *We*: two well-meaning people who wanted something from the other that the other could not give.

I kissed the man whose sweater smelled like dog.

"I'll stay here tonight, if it's okay, but I'm not in a place to get involved with you. I still love my wife."

"Yeah, I know you do. I think you should go."

It cut me to say it, to send him away, but I had long before learned it was unwise to have sex with a man who did not belong to me.

I walked with him into the light drizzle.

"Please tell me you'll take good care of yourself," I said. We exchanged a quick hug and a kiss. I watched Sam run down my street towards town and his friend's loft above the noodle shop. Afterwards, I went inside and switched off the porch light.

Three weeks after I'd first met Sam, I did it again: I went out on the town of San Luis Obispo by myself. I ventured forth, buoyed with the hope of reliving my serendipitous encounter with Sam—hoping to discover a man who could conjure magic similar to what Sam and I had shared. I was an addict chasing a former high.

But twenty-one days prior it had been summer. When I stepped from my car that second time, I knew fall had descended. The wind, infamous and persistent in SLO, was present that night, yet the merrymakers were not. Dried leaves, dirt, and small scraps of paper flurried in dust devils on top of the vacant sidewalks. Sam wasn't at Frog & Peach, so I didn't stay. I wondered how he, his misguided wife, and their children were faring.

Dressed in a sleeveless mini and high heels, I was chilled. I ducked into a swanky bar, drank a glass of wine, and exited. I sat at a wrought-iron patio table in front of a gourmet deli and ate a slice of pesto and artichoke pizza. It had been sitting under the deli case's warming lights, but they hadn't done the trick—pizza rigor mortis had set in. I headed for home in my getaway car.

I've returned to dating online because I learned that discovering love in "real life" does not lack drawbacks. I suppose that all avenues leading to love are fraught with various roadblocks.

The lessons I've gleaned from my nights out solo are simple gems of great value to me. They included taking stock in the mirror to acknowledge that, even with the passing of the years, this old girl's still got it. I dared to reach beyond my comfort zone—without any guarantees—toward the pursuit of unknown adventure. I celebrated my small successes with gusto, and I lassoed the resiliency to rebound from my disappointments. If my main task was to arrive at a place where I honored my own needs—which included recognizing when I should refrain from my momentary desires—I believe I handled myself with aplomb. No speedy getaway necessary.

He Lost Me at Hello

First Dates That Were Last Dates

- My sixty-year-old date arrived with a portfolio of him as a nineteen-year-old model. He fanned his pics on top of our dinner table and commenced to discuss his youthful good looks.

- He removed his shoe and massaged his foot underneath the restaurant table—then suggested we share a bowl of Thai noodles.

- It was obvious my date had falsified his profile statistics. He'd lied about his age, height, weight, and eye color. Why would anybody lie about their eye color?

- As we said good-bye in the parking lot, he proceeded to run his hand up my thigh and underneath my skirt.

- My date admitted he was politically conservative rather than "middle of the road" as he'd stated in his online profile. He confessed he'd stretched the truth to gain easier access to liberal pussy.

- When I asked him what he did for exercise, he said he'd like to rub against me.

- His favorite film was *Dumb and Dumber*.

- My date said he hadn't obtained a divorce because he'd rather eat lobster three nights a week than pay the legal fees to dissolve his marriage.

- He confessed he wore a toupee. I've nothing against bald men, only toupees.

- He educated me on the difference between "Blacks" and "Niggers."

- He called his high-school-aged daughter each night to sing her to sleep.

- I was his first postdivorce date. He asked if I'd be willing to "help him out" with his first postdivorce sex.

- His profile had stated he didn't smoke. From across the table, his raunchy cigarette breath accosted me.

- He recounted the release dates of every Beatles album—ever.

- He told me his father lived in an old school bus and bathed twice a year. I worried my date might be a chip off the old (engine) block.

- I thought our conversation was progressing well—until he stopped midsentence to tell me he'd been staring at my "tits."

- He did not smile. Not once.

- He said he was attracted to women with large dark-pigmented areolae. My areolae are small to medium. Pinkish.

- My date checked out every woman who walked into Starbucks.

- He said that if I wanted to know more about him, I could log on to YouTube where he'd posted his life story. When we stood in line to order our tea, he told the barista the same thing.

- He'd been married three times and had eight kids—a *wee* detail my date had failed to mention in his profile.

- He said that if he were the stalker type, he would stalk me.

- My date accused me of being rude and inconsiderate when I arrived four minutes late.

- Multiple times during our tasty meal, he remarked that his mouth was having (multiple) orgasms.

- My date said his penis resembled a toggle light switch in its diminutive size and quick up-down operation. Enlightening information, indeed.

Man-Kiss

I WAS NEW IN TOWN, YET AT THE SAME TIME, I'D COME HOME. I had recently relocated to my native city after sixteen years away. Indian summer had brought a sharp vividness to Santa Barbara's gossamer beauty and had blasted her with furnace-like heat. It felt wonderful to be back.

Paul was a Santa Barbara local whom I met on the Plenty Of Fish dating site at the time of my move. During our first phone conversation, I noticed an airy quality to his voice. He sounded effeminate. I value males who are comfortable expressing their feminine side—who possess *a touch of lavender.* The timbre of Paul's voice had registered as insignificant. I'd not been in the mood to nitpick.

Paul invited me to join him for wine tasting on Stearns Wharf. After I handed my car keys to the pier's valet, I went in search of Paul. I found him where he'd said he would be, standing beneath the shop sign: Madame Rosinka, Palm Reader. As a girl, I'd been told that my palm foretold a long life. I had no idea what it said about how I'd be fated in love. Paul was ten years my junior and a husky six feet tall, with broad meaty shoulders, short curly blonde hair, and piercing blue eyes. When I approached, he gave me a warm hug and told me I was pretty.

My date and I sought shade beneath an umbrella perched outside a small wine bar. We sipped chardonnay—beads of condensation clinging to our glasses—alongside dozens of people who'd come to the ocean seeking relief from the heat. Our smiles and laughter bubbled effortlessly. As we talked, I touched Paul's arm.

Following wine, we walked the length of the wharf in the direction of downtown. Paul placed his hand on the small of my back to guide me through a throng of tourists. We ended up at the Funk Zone: a popular pocket of shops, avant-garde artist studios, and bistros located a few blocks from the beach. Our first kiss was outside a gourmet pizza shop called Lucky Penny—its copper facade aglow in the setting sun. I had to stand on my tiptoes with my head tilted back. No fireworks ensued, but there were adequate sparks. Paul suggested we sit at the bar and order a pizza. Although I prefer spicy toppings, he selected a variety garnished with fresh fig. We each had another glass of wine.

"Our bartender is pretty, isn't he?" said Paul.

"Yes, he is." Peculiar. I'd been thinking the same thing.

I couldn't shrug it off any longer—his subtle feminine mannerisms, the slight swish of his walk, the shallow breathiness of his speech. Fig pizza. I took a sip (swig) of wine. And then, I took (Ferdinand) the bull by his horns.

"Paul, I know you were married, but do you think you're gay? Or bisexual?"

"No, I'm not gay, but I've kissed a guy."

"Really? Do tell."

"When I was in my twenties, my gay friend and I got drunk. He asked me if I'd ever kissed a man. I said no, so my friend suggested I kiss him—to see how it felt."

I squirmed a little on my barstool. My palms began to sweat. "And?"

"I didn't like it. My friend's stubble scratched my face."

Apparently it wasn't the swapping of tongues and saliva that Paul had found distasteful, but the dude's stubble. A quick close shave would have remedied that pesky irritation, and Paul and his friend could have given their man-kiss another whirl. Maybe they did.

I felt queasy. My right temple began to throb. I'd never encountered anything like this. Being a woman among attractive women was pressure enough; however, if that wasn't enough for me to contend with, there was this: it was possible my date lusted after both sexes. I knew there was no way I could compete with the "prettiness" of our stunning young bartender. Paul retained not a touch of lavender, but a bushel. I was out of my league.

We ate our fig pizza (yuck!), and Paul left our bartender a lavish tip. Then, surprisingly, Paul asked me out again. Despite my insecurities, I said yes.

For date number two, we met at the beach. Paul brought his dog–a tiny dog on a tiny leash. While he held his dog's leash, Paul raised his right forearm, bent his wrist, and dropped his hand forward, just so. We walked on the beach and sat on a rock to kiss. Then Paul asked if I'd like to go shopping with him.

The next morning Paul picked me up in his Land Cruiser and we cruised south to Nordstrom Rack. Paul selected several T-shirts and tried them on. He gazed at himself in the full-length mirror, turned sideways, then back to center. He petted his chest and torso in long repetitive strokes, smoothing the already snug-fitting material. I encouraged Paul to purchase a pink silk dress shirt and a black dinner jacket that looked striking on his tall hunky frame. We walked by the jewelry counter.

"I like that gold watch with the bold face," I said. "It would look great with your new pink shirt."

"Oh no. I always wear silver. If I bought that watch I would have to mix my metals. I don't like to mix my metals."

I knew what Paul meant, but how many *men* would know, or care, that mixing metals could be considered a fashion faux pas? Paul bought me several pairs of panties he'd selected, and I bought him a scented candle for his bedroom. Then we did lunch.

Paul and I had fun together, and we seemed to have a lot in common. He and I had the same taste in men, I rarely mix metals (or when I do, it pains me), and I liked hanging out with him and his small dog, on her small leash. Paul kept asking me out and I kept saying yes. We had sex one time. Paul's face became very red with the effort, and I worried his heart would come unglued—not the typical organ to come unglued during sex. He brought me to orgasm, although I was not able to return him the favor.

Following a two-week whirlwind romance, Paul called me one evening to break things off.

"Rebecca, I really like you, and I've enjoyed our time together, but I want to meet a woman I can conceive a child with."

I fought back tears. I'm a big sissy whilst being dumped.

"I had a feeling this would come up. You told me that a year ago you broke up with a woman for that exact reason."

"I would like to reposition you from girlfriend status to 'the friend zone.'"

Perhaps Paul envisioned us hanging out together in the friend zone—shopping for clothes and accessorizing appropriately— while he continued to search the web for his baby mama. I'd been demoted.

I sniffled. My lower lip trembled. I needed to get off the phone, and fast.

"I appreciate your generous offer, Paul, but no thanks. That's not what I'm looking for."

I credit Paul for being man enough to call and break up with me, instead of simply disappearing without a trace, which is common practice for a lot of guys. I never saw Paul again, but I've enjoyed the panties he bought me, and I hope he has enjoyed his candle. I've wondered if he has discovered a suitable partner with whom he could have a child. I think it unfortunate for Paul that Ricky Martin and Neil Patrick Harris are both happily married with children.

You Can't Judge an Angel by His Name

*G*OOD MORNING! *Aren't we the lucky ones to live in Santa Barbara?*
~Rebecca

Hello there. Thanks for initiating contact. Judging from your written profile and pics I can tell you are just the kind of woman I'm looking for. Please tell me a little more about yourself and what you're seeking from this site. I hope to hear from you soon so we can arrange a time to meet. Fondly, Angelo

"Fondly." Really? Isn't that a tad over the top considering he doesn't know me? Perhaps I've evoked Angelo's undue fondness because he and I both live in Santa Barbara. No, that's probably not it. I think he's fond of me because I began my email with a cheery "Good morning!" My old Nana was right. A shining attitude is always a sure bet.

Hi Angelo! I contacted you because you live in my city, are close to my age, are single (the most important factor ;-)), and I liked your written profile and photo. You're handsome, but I wish you had posted more than one pic. I am a Santa Barbara native. I've recently returned to my hometown to be closer to my elderly father. I've sold my property in San Luis Obispo and I'm allowing myself a year to focus on writing a book. I subscribe to Plenty Of Fish because I hope to establish a long-term relationship with a great guy. Have a wonderful day! ~Rebecca

Hey Babe. Fantastic to hear back from you! I feel we share closeness, although we've not met. I was an only child born to missionary parents. I had a very lonely childhood. Three years ago my wife and mother died in a fiery car crash. At the time my wife was killed, we were trying to start a family. I was devastated of course, but now I am fully recovered and eager to find love again. Please leave me your phone number and I will call you. You are beautiful inside and out. Fondly, Angelo

A fiery car crash? How unbelievably grim. Poor Angelo! I feel such compassion for him. But apart from that, he thinks I'm special. He's right. I *am* special! He is a handsome, sad man who recognizes my worth. I will definitely email him my cell number. He'll call, we will meet, and soon after, fall in love and be married. He will be a father figure to my son, Max. Max needs a consistent male influence in his life. But I wonder why Angelo called me "Babe?" That part seems a little weird. I know, it's probably because he's Italian. Italian men are uncommonly demonstrative.

Hello Angelo. Please accept my sincere condolences for the tragic loss of your wife and mother. I think you're very brave to venture forth to seek love again. I'll leave you my cell number, and you can call anytime, but most nights after eight work best. I have a son, and he's usually in bed by that time. Oh, btw, it's my policy to insist on at least one date before I'll allow a man to call me Babe ;-) ~Rebecca (805) 999-9999

Angelo didn't call before eight, or any time after eight.

Hi Babe. My father and mother were visiting the states when she was killed. Following her death, my father returned to Africa to continue his ministry. I've just received news he is very ill. I'll be flying out of Santa Barbara today. I hope I'm able to get to my father's bedside in time. I will email you every day. Promise me you'll not date anybody else. I want us to be together. Fondly, Angelo

That explains why Angelo hasn't called! He's had a major family emergency!

Hi Angelo. Thank you for letting me know about your father's illness and your travels to Africa to be with him. What a loving and dutiful son you are. Although I appreciate your sincerity toward me, please remember that you and I have yet to meet, or even to speak on the phone. Most guys resist becoming exclusive even after they've gotten to know a woman, but you, my friend, want to commit before we've heard one another's voices! Are you a real person? Have a good trip. I'm certain you'll make it in time. ~Rebecca

You ask if I am a real person? Why are you so jaded and mistrusting? I want to be with you because you are kind and deep and caring. But now you are suspicious that I'm withholding the truth! I arrived in Africa yesterday. My father is very sick but still alive. I've come back to my room for a shower and change of clothes before returning to the hospital to be with him. *The native people stare at me because I am a tall, blonde, white man. Africa is a strange country. Angelo*

I must have really pissed him off. Angelo didn't address me as "Babe," or close with "Fondly."

Hey Angelo. It was never my intention to insult you. It's just that sometimes your emails sound as if they could be directed towards anybody, not specifically me. I'm a woman who wants to remain open to dating strangers, but at the same time, it's necessary I watch out for myself. I hope you can understand. Don't worry about emailing me. Please spend as much time as possible with your dad. ~Rebecca

Babe. My father has died. It's so stressful for me to be in a foreign country while attempting to make funeral arrangements. Burial ground is expensive here. I'm unsure whether I should bury my father in Africa or fly his body back to the States. Either option is very costly. Fondly, Angelo

Hello Angelo. I'm sorry to hear about the death of your father. I know it was a great comfort for him to have you by his side. Have you considered asking your father's church to help with the financial burden of burial costs? I'm sure he was well loved and respected. Others will offer you their assistance on your father's behalf. ~Rebecca

Babe. Will you loan me money for my father's burial? I will pay you back when I return to Santa Barbara. Fondly, Angelo

Dear Angelo. Like your father before you, drop dead! Fondly, Babe

His Square Peg

I HAD ASSUMED OUR ONLINE CONNECTION HAD FIZZLED. Then out of the blue he called. Twice. The first time I'd been in the shower. He'd left no message. Twenty minutes later, as I was toweling off, he called again.

"Hi. This is Seth from Plenty Of Fish."

"Wow! I'm kinda surprised to hear from you! What's up?"

"You were persistent about us meeting, and you left me your number, so I figured I'd call."

Seth was right about my persistence. From the time I'd first come across his profile, I knew I wanted to meet him. I liked that his description of himself and his lifestyle was average guy-ish, not pervy, or boastful, or apathetic. He shared custody of a son my son's age. His photos showed more effort than selfies, yet they weren't the over-the-top studio variety either. I was looking for a normal guy. Seth had appeared exceedingly normal.

I'd emailed Seth. He responded. I emailed him again. I received no further response, but I wrote him anyway—and I left my phone number. I should've known better. I *had* known better. But I did it nonetheless.

"It's been two weeks since I emailed you my number. I didn't expect to hear from you."

"To tell you the truth, I was a little hesitant. You're older than most of the women I date."

"Don't worry, Seth, I'm no dried-up old biddy."

I wasn't, was I? My pride would not let me go there.

"Would you like to go for a walk on Hendry's Beach tomorrow at three o'clock? I'll meet you at the lifeguard tower."

"That sounds great. I look forward to it. See you then!"

He seemed *nice*.

The beach was gorgeous. The sun was silver glitter on the water. White canvas sails bloomed from the ocean's surface like water lilies, and the Channel Islands, thirty miles offshore, were minus their usual blanket of fog. Beachcombers strolled the coastline with their canine companions, college coeds tossed Frisbees, and bronze bikini-clad women were prone on colorful beach towels.

As we'd agreed, I met Seth at the lifeguard tower at three o'clock. If he hadn't told me exactly where he'd be waiting, I wouldn't have recognized Seth as the athletic man in his profile photos. In person, Seth was weighted with an ample spare tire that protruded beneath his loose-fitting cotton shirt. When he smiled to greet me, I noticed Seth's teeth were stained gopher yellow. His jaws worked a wad of gum.

But I was at the beach, the weather was glorious, and I was determined not to judge Seth by my first lackluster impression. I wanted to focus on other things besides his looks. I wanted to give this man a chance.

I could clear the hurdle of Seth's physical shortcomings, but there were larger issues. "Damn girl, you're hot!" he exclaimed as

I approached. His comment was a bad sign. Relationship-minded men do not make sexually forward comments on the first date. Well-intentioned men take their time. On this otherwise bright day, Seth was a dark cloud that forebodes a storm.

As we walked the length of the beach, Seth made it repeatedly clear: *I* was the reason the beach was hot. His comments made me self-conscious, but I tried to joke them off.

"I had no idea I wielded such atmospheric influence! Maybe we should contact weatherman Al Roker. If it's me determining the temperature, I think I deserve nationwide recognition!"

Seth was undeterred. He slung his beefy left arm around my shoulder and stuck his right hand down my top. I batted him away. A woman in a large sunhat and long pants rolled to her calves approached us from the opposite direction. As we passed, I appealed to her for sympathy.

"Excuse me, ma'am. Judging from this guy's behavior, how long do you think we've known each other?"

"I don't know, but you two sure look like you're having fun!"

Fun? Really? Is that what I looked like I was having? Maybe she meant fun as in fun-house fun—which is bizarre and distorted, and honestly, no fun at all.

My car, left behind in the sand-dusted parking lot, seemed miles away. In my imagination, my humble Scion xD became a Ferrari, a stretch limo, a taxi, an ambulance—waiting to whisk me away from my bad judgment, and far away from my bad-news date.

By four o'clock, Seth had attempted to fondle every part of my body legally allowable in a public setting. He was not interested in talk. Whenever I'd initiate conversation, Seth would respond with parrotlike responses.

"Are you always so frisky on a first date?" I asked.

"Oh, so you think I'm frisky, huh?"

"Yes! Please keep your hands to the outermost regions of my northern hemisphere!"

Seth pulled me over to him, told me he wanted to kiss me, and then did so. His mouth tasted of overripe watermelon and rodent teeth. I wiped away his residue with the back of my hand.

"If I tripped and fell in the sand, I think you'd take it as an invitation to jump my bones!"

"Oh, so you think I want to jump your bones, huh?"

"Yes, I do! Did you happen to drink several shots of whiskey before our date?"

"Oh, so you think I drank whiskey, huh?"

"Yes! And I think you're chewing watermelon gum to disguise the smell!"

I had extended my good graces for long enough. There was no way to redeem this date. When we had returned to the parking lot I made a beeline for my car. Neither of us said good-bye. In spite of the beautiful day, I felt blue.

I recognized I had gone overboard to make an online connection with Seth. Foolishly, I'd attempted to fit a square peg into a round hole; I'd forced the attentions of a man who was an impossible fit. Because I had pushed for us to meet, my date had assumed I would be an easy score. Seth entertained high hopes that I'd allow him to put his "peg" into my "hole."

Pollyanna
Goes to Tea

A SWARM OF BICYCLISTS braked at The Coffee Bean & Tea Leaf and parked their bikes out front. A middle-aged man dismounted, removed his helmet, and strolled past the outdoor table where Kenny and I sat. His cycling shoes made a rhythmic *click-clack* on the concrete walkway as he journeyed toward hot java. Kenny halted our conversation midsentence, sprang from his seat, embraced the man, and then introduced me to his friend Ted. Ted had been in Kenny's "club." Unbeknownst to me, I had just received a peek into a secret society I'd not known existed until tea.

Kenny was a commissioned Navy officer who'd recently been promoted to a high-ranking position. He and I met for tea in Carpinteria—home of the world's safest beach—a halfway point from our towns of residence. I had once deemed it preferable that an out-of-town suitor drive to my city for our first date, but I've since altered my position. The majority of first dates secured from

online connections are a bust. I no longer want to shoulder the responsibility of insisting a man travel to meet me, only to discover we are a poor fit. Nowadays, I offer to rendezvous at a location that's equidistant for both.

Prior to our tea date, Kenny and I spoke on the phone and exchanged a series of text messages. Kenny had been open with me about the fact he was polyamorous. I'd had to Google it. A polyamorous individual is involved with more than one person at a time. That seemed reasonable. In that case, I was polyamorous too. Weren't we all, until we discovered "the one?"

As Ted walked away, Kenny and I returned to our chat. I removed my lightweight cardigan sweater and laid it across my lap. Unless I intervened with needle and thread, my sweater would lose a button. In a row of taut ones, a delicate mother-of-pearl disk hung limply, attached to the garment by a single smoke-colored fiber. My exposed arms soaked up the gentle midafternoon sun. The fragrant tea and the warm sunshine contributed to my sense of tranquility. Suddenly sleepy, I stifled a yawn. I looked across the table at my date. Kenny was a decent-looking fellow three years my junior: tall, more pepper than salt, a T-shirt and jeans kind of guy, a bit soft in the paunch—a condition common to men over forty-five. So far, he hadn't wowed me, but regardless, I figured he'd be harmless company for midday tea.

Kenny sat back in his chair, put both hands behind his head—transforming his arms into two scalene triangles—and without further ceremony, brought his sexual fetishes to light.

"Late one night, I was drinking beer and channel surfing when I happened upon a program about S&M. That show changed my life."

My serene mood disappeared like water down the drain. I sat on the edge of my seat. My sweater slid from my lap and landed on a grimy glob of gum beneath our table. The sun scorched my shoulders and I scalded my tongue on too-hot tea. I rallied with a wisecrack, my modus operandi when I feel uncomfortable.

"What if you'd happened upon a televised Billy Graham revival, instead? It makes me shudder to think where you might be today." I'm such a smartass.

My joke whizzed by him—undetected or ignored? Kenny continued.

"Polyamory is a venue for normal sexual expression. When I started experimenting with more than one sexual partner, I was amazed to discover how many people were looking for the same thing. That's why I decided to start a club where adults from our area could gather to engage in alternative types of sex, including sadomasochism and bondage."

I tried to be open. I tried to empathize with Kenny and his promiscuous tendencies. I tried to imagine what a polyamory meeting might be like—

Following the club minutes, naked men and women would break into small groups. (Was the person who'd been picked last for group sports in grade school picked last for group sex too?) Members would take turns handcuffing one another to bedposts, tickling their neighbor with feathers, and spanking a participant who'd been a "very bad boy." In the name of propriety, I hoped Kenny kept the clubhouse lights on dimmers, or that the softness of candlelight was utilized. A middle-aged orgy staged under unforgiving fluorescent lights would be far from pretty.

Question: How had it come to pass that I sat sipping steeped chamomile with a man who clamored for whips and chains?

Never had it been my intention to welcome weirdos aboard my Good Ship Lollipop, but they'd stowed themselves there, nevertheless.

Like my sixty-four-year-old gynecologist. The same day he'd performed my annual pap smear, he had contacted me via Match.com to ask me out. I said no, of course—how creepy! But apparently, I'm still lookin' good down there.

Holding his cup in both hands, Kenny propped his elbows on the table and leaned across it, taking me into his confidence. "I've recently had to shut down the club so I could obtain government clearance for my job promotion. My hope is that attitudes are changing. Someday the Navy will express tolerance for the practice of polyamory."

"Yeah, I can see that happening. And maybe the Pope will jump on the bandwagon."

The coffeehouse door opened and I saw Ted exit. He walked past our table—*click-clack, click-clack*. He and Kenny exchanged a thumbs-up.

"Rebecca, I would consider giving up my lifestyle should you choose to date me. To be honest, polyamory isn't an easy sell in the majority of dating circles. I've discovered it's not the average woman's cup of tea." Kenny chuckled at his cleverness and lifted his heat-resistant cup in a celebratory toast. I retrieved my sweater and slipped it on. An iridescent button dangled third from the top. I regarded my date.

"It's challenge enough to forge a monogamous relationship with a man. What fool would date the founder of a club that catered to kinky sex with multiple partners? Not this fool!"

I hadn't really said that to Kenny. As Nancy Reagan once advised, I just said no. *No* was all that was needed. *No* sufficed. Then, I said good-bye to my polyamorous friend and drove my Pollyanna-morous self home.

A Woman Walks into a Bar . . .

A HIGHLY SOUGHT COMMODITY ON THE DATING SCENE? Wittiness. A "good sense of humor" is often listed at the forefront of men and women's online "must-haves." Also popular must-haves: somebody who likes to hike or take long walks on the beach. From my own daily treks, I've discovered that rural trails in Santa Barbara are not teeming with eligible singles, nor is the beach. Perhaps if individuals who claim they desire such a partner frequented local trails and neighboring beaches themselves, there'd be no further need for dating sites.

People will request that which they're not able to deliver. Many seek a sense of humor in another, yet they're ill-equipped to return the favor. Funny people are an endangered species.

I had trouble securing street parking near Blush Restaurant + Lounge, where Robert had suggested we meet. I called Robert to tell him I was searching for a spot a block from the restaurant, and that it was likely I'd be a few minutes late. We continued talking as Robert walked outside the restaurant to flag me into the parking garage on Ortega Street.

I drove in Robert's direction and he remained standing on the sidewalk adjacent to the garage. I waved as I went past. My first impression? *Ooh, he's cute!* I pulled into the garage, quickly located a space, and hurried outside to the sidewalk where I anticipated Robert would be waiting. He wasn't. I walked into Blush and spoke with the hostess. She directed me to the patio. Robert was already seated at the outdoor bar, enjoying a glass of red wine.

Judging from his outward appearance, fifty-four-year-old Robert should have been dynamite with the ladies. He was tall, he was dark, he was well dressed, and he was handsome. He'd been blessed with thick, shiny hair, broad shoulders, and smooth unblemished skin. Match.com had got it right this time. The site had matched me with Robert.

I extended my hand. "Hi Robert, I'm Rebecca. I was worried you'd caught sight of me as I drove by and decided to split." I laughed as I said this, though honestly, I'd been perplexed, and slightly wounded, by my date's disappearing act.

"No, of course I didn't leave. I would *never* do that. But yeah, maybe I should've waited for you and we could've walked in together."

Do ya think?

A man who was aware of the importance of basic social decorum would have waited for me as I parked my car. That act alone— *waiting*—would have served as a blind-date icebreaker. It would've offered Robert and me the opportunity to bond over a shared adventure, regardless of how small or insignificant it appeared. Robert's failure to pick up on subtle social cues tallied a strike against him.

I put it behind me and sat on the barstool next to Robert. He smelled nice—Abercrombie?

"What are you drinking?" I asked.

"Per Bacco Cellars Pinot Noir. It's excellent."

"Per Bacco, huh? Of course it's excellent! Bacchus is the god of wine. If you can't trust a wine god to make excellent wine, who *can* you trust?"

Robert furrowed his brow. He looked confused—not amused. I watched as my wisecrack soared over Robert's luxurious and manly perfumed head. Maybe it was me. Maybe my timing was off. I rallied. And piped down.

"I'll have what you're having."

Our time together was nice enough, although I'd had to carry the conversation. I didn't mind. The more difficult task was coming to terms with the fact that strapping six-foot-two Robert had been born with a midget-sized funny bone. Robert seemed like an individual who required an interpreter to tell him when something witty had been said: "That was supposed to be a joke," or, "Hey, I'm just teasing you."

Maybe Robert didn't want to take the chance his humor (or lack thereof) would come out wrong—to have others laugh *at* him instead of *with* him. Perhaps Robert wanted to make certain he would never overstep the bounds of propriety and chuckle at an ill-mannered joke or bust out laughing in an inopportune moment. Maybe he preferred to minimize risk and play it safe. I wanted to believe that Robert was simply *comically cautious*. But after thirty minutes together, it became clear: humor was not his native language.

But that's not to imply he wasn't a good catch. Robert *was* a good catch. He showed up on time. He paid for my glass of wine and

tasty appetizers. He was far from pretentious. He was well groomed. He smelled sublime. *And,* Robert owned a home in pricey Santa Barbara, which is no easy accomplishment. Robert was responsible. Responsible people are an endangered species too.

To be (responsible), *or not to be* (funny)? That was the question I needed to consider. I would enjoy being paired with a man who is quietly funny, or playfully so, but I'm not ignorant to the art of compromise. I understand that traits like honesty, loyalty, and steadfastness are important too. Perhaps it's unrealistic for me to believe that creative mirth deserves top billing. Maybe scoring a man with an evolved sense of humor was grossly overrated.

Following our date, Robert texted to say he'd had a good time. Then, I didn't hear from him for three months. Ninety days after our first date, Robert texted to say hello and to ask me out. Too much time had passed, and I'd lost all interest in him. I responded, *No thx :-(*

Buuut then . . . six months after our first date, I came across Robert's profile on Match.com. His pics were great. He had such a nice smile. He looked so handsome in his group photos—and so socially participatory. Maybe *I* was the one who required an interpreter. Maybe I had misread Robert. I emailed him. Robert responded and asked me to join him at Blush for a glass of wine. I accepted.

This time I was prepared. I parked my car in a space at the Ortega Street garage, and I waited for Robert at the restaurant entrance. Robert approached. He looked wonderful. He smelled amazing. It was good to see him.

"Hi, Robert! When we met here last time, I missed my opportunity to walk into Blush with you. Today I was smart. I got here early to guarantee I wouldn't miss out again!"

"I'm sorry, Rebecca. I didn't know I was late."

"You're *not* late. I was making a joke. I was *flirting* with you."

Robert hadn't changed. His funny bone hadn't experienced a growth spurt, but I'd been prepared for that as well. Perhaps Robert's straightforward approach to life would be of benefit to me: a woman with witty remarks ready and waiting on the tip of her tongue. Maybe sensible Robert would prove an effective tonic for my verbal shenanigans.

Robert and I walked into Blush together. It felt nice to walk into a restaurant with a man. Most of the meals I've shared with men occurred on first (and only) dates. Usually, when I've agreed to meet a new man at a restaurant, we arrive separately, and several minutes apart. Most of the time I walk in alone. But Robert and I were having our second date. We had a shared history. We were practically an old married couple.

It was five o'clock and winter—a chilly sixty-five degrees. We sat at the inside bar.

"Thanks for asking me out when I emailed you on Match yesterday. Since you didn't call or text for three months after our first date, I figured you weren't into me."

"I didn't wait three months to contact you, Rebecca! Give me a minute to review my text messages. I'll double-check the exact date." Robert picked up his phone. He traveled back in time.

Hmm . . . He'd actually kept my text messages from six months ago? I hadn't kept his. When a man I'm seeing doesn't pan out, I'll swiftly delete his contact information, his voicemails, and his text messages. *Out with the old, in with the new:* that's my motto.

"Yes, Rebecca, you're right! It *was* three months from the time of our first date before I asked you out again. I've been traveling a lot for work."

Ah, yes—traveling, traveling, traveling—with nary a reprieve. Silly

of me to expect more. I forgive you, Robert. After all, you can't help it that you're a socially inept engineer. I knew better than to say that. I held my tongue.

"I want to be truthful with you," said Robert. "I've been recovering from a breakup. I fell in love with a Brazilian woman who left me to finish school in Los Angeles. She's been gone a month. We still talk some, but she's no longer interested in me."

"She went to LA to go to *school?* How old is she?"

"She's sixteen years younger than me. Maybe that was part of the problem."

I laughed, although Robert wasn't making a joke. I find humor in all the wrong places.

He showed me her photo. She looked like the Mona Lisa. Historians insist Mona had been a beauty, but even after taking a class in art appreciation, I still couldn't see it.

For the next forty-five minutes, I sat on a barstool and listened to Robert wax poetic about his lost woman from Brazil. I've always been a sympathetic listener, so I was mostly happy to do it. But right then and there, I mentally erased Robert from my (waning) list of eligible male prospects.

If a man is out with a woman, and all he does is talk about his ex, it's nothing short of bad manners. But on this particular occasion, I was relieved. And grateful. Prior to my second date with Robert, I'd stood at a crossroad. I had considered whether I'd be willing to forfeit my dream of a jocular mate and settle for a stilted man who offered stability. Now I didn't have to choose. The choice had been made for me.

I finished my wine. I made no jokes. Robert told me he liked me. He thanked me for listening. Then, he asked me for advice on how to get his girlfriend back.

Oh, brother!

Maybe a reasonable woman would have been insulted, but I wasn't. I cannot resist giving personal advice. Especially when it's solicited.

"Either you could end all contact with her and hope she'll miss you enough to come back, or you could show up on her front porch in LA and make a heroic appeal for her love. I kinda favor the idea of you making a dramatic scene on her stoop."

He looked pitiful. "What if she sends me away?"

"She might. There's no way to know that beforehand. When you put your pride on the line for a woman, it's romantic—and exciting. It's called *passion*. Chicks dig it."

I had become bored of Robert's Brazilian. I opted for a change of pace.

"I have an idea," I said. "Bath & Body Works in Paseo Nuevo is having a sale on candles. I'm going to buy a few. Do you want to come with me to sniff candles?"

He was sulky. His eyes looked sad. Two glasses of wine had not buoyed his spirits.

"Sure, I'll go. But I won't buy anything."

"I understand that. You're coming along simply for the *fun* of it."

Robert and I walked across the street to the outdoor mall: a Mediterranean wonderland. We were greeted by a multitude of whitewashed shops with red tile roofs, brick walkways, architectural arches, fountains, stairs faced with hand-painted Mexican tiles, and an abundance of blossoming plants that cascaded over the rims of huge ceramic pots. We entered Bath & Body Works.

A salesgirl directed me to the display of three-wick candles. I removed the thin metal lids from a variety of candles, closed my eyes, and inhaled their fragrances: Hawaiian Beach, Oahu Coconut

Sunset, Hawaii Passionfruit Kiss. Robert stood at my side with his hands in his pockets. In an attempt to coax a smile from him, I positioned a candle under his nose.

"Smell this. It's called *Brazilian* Beach." I picked up another candle. "Here's one called *Brazilian* Coconut Sunset, and another called *Brazilian* Passionfruit Kiss."

Judging from the look on Robert's face, I'd done something horrific. My candle caper was supposed to tickle his funny bone—diminutive as it was—instead, I'd struck a raw nerve.

"Rebecca, you're making fun of me! I don't think you're the least bit amusing! I've got to go!"

"I'm sorry to have hurt your feelings. I was only trying to lighten things up."

Robert stormed out. Unencumbered now, I bought six candles—two for the price of one. Brazil for the low cost of Hawaii.

The Legal Ramifications of Kiss Avoidance

IMPRISONED IN A GLASS AND VINYL TOMB known as the backseat of a police car, I held on to a thin fiber of composure, like the stray thread that clung to the flirty hem of my summer dress. I wanted nothing more than to pull my black cardigan sweater around me like a protective cocoon, yet under the circumstances, that otherwise simple task was hopelessly impossible.

Minutes earlier, my hands had been shackled behind my back with metal cuffs. Now those handcuffs had begun to feel more than a little uncomfortable. Especially the left one. The tight steel bracelet pressed itself painfully into the unpadded flesh of my bony wrist. Void of fresh air and separated from the driver's seat by a section of bulletproof glass, the tight space of the prisoner's cab closed in on me like the encroaching walls of a TV villain's torture chamber.

I experienced an unexpected wave of compassion for all detainees everywhere, who at that very moment were also confined to the backseats of squad cars. I felt special pity for culprits of the obese variety. If my petite five-foot-one frame was uncomfortable, I couldn't fathom how a portly individual could possibly fit into such a restricted space.

I focused on the solitary act of inhaling a measured stream of stale air. I held it, then released. I willed away the claustrophobia that threatened to wrap my mind in a suffocating blanket. I was acutely aware of how easily panic could overwhelm me should I allow my shaky resolve to slip by a single degree. I ordered myself not to cry. At age fifty-six, I knew crying would only make things worse. I knew tears would melt away my courage like sugar in the rain.

I stared outward at the bustling Santa Barbara nightlife. My native city's main street was hopping. I witnessed people strolling by in groups of two or more, arms linked, heads thrown back, engaged in laughter and lively conversation. My local compatriots appeared neither curious nor concerned about the blonde middle-aged woman handcuffed in the back of a patrol car parked at the curb. Perhaps it was then I first took serious stock of my unfortunate plight. How could it be remotely possible that my first date with a nice enough fellow had ended with me in such a compromised state? And speaking of my date, where the hell had that nice enough fellow disappeared to?

Steven and I had been introduced via the popular Plenty Of Fish dating site. I had initiated contact, and he'd responded. Most online encounters quickly fizzle, yet Steven and I'd moved forward to exchange cell numbers. We had spoken a couple of times on the phone, and he'd arranged a date with me for Friday. He'd offered to drive from

Malibu to Santa Barbara after work traffic subsided, and we'd planned to meet near the corner of Ortega and State Street at eight-thirty. In advance, we'd decided to walk State Street, get acquainted, and then choose a place where we would enjoy a late dinner. As I approached the sidewalk bench where Steven waited, he stood and greeted me with a warm hug. In person Steven was every bit as animated as he had exhibited through text messages and phone conversations. He was well groomed, courteous, and enthusiastic about the night at hand. Talk flowed easily between us. As we walked by the restaurant Killer Shrimp, Steven recommended it with fervor. He'd eaten there before and insisted the restaurant served "the best shrimp ever." Once we'd been seated, I ordered a chardonnay and Steven requested an iced tea. True to his word, the shrimp were tasty. I offered to help with the check, but Steven commandeered with old-fashioned aplomb.

Unhurried, my date and I strolled the several blocks to the beach, and then ventured onto Stearns Wharf. The night was noticeably cool, as is typical for Santa Barbara, even in high summer. Steven and I sat on a rough-hewn bench positioned atop the shop-peppered wharf. Restaurant patrons had retired their tables to the closing help, and only they lingered, sweeping up remnants of the evening's festivities. At that time of night, Steven and I had only each other for company, and the night air, perfumed with a woeful hint of brine and the petrol scent of creosote. Steven shared that he aspired to produce a private film, and to father a child—a wee one, he said, to whom he would pass his chiseled jaw and baby blues.

It seemed unlikely that Steven's dreams could somehow mesh with mine. I had four older children and a grandbaby. Weathering toddler tantrums, hosing vomit from bedsheets, and driving a purple mom-van were miseries I'd gratefully consigned to my long-ago. I looked at the dark ocean. I placed my hands in my lap. Time and motherhood had robbed them of their beauty.

"I want to kiss you," Steven said. He scooted closer and placed his right hand over mine.

"No hurry," I said. "I believe in taking baby steps." What I thought was, *Whoa there, cowboy!*

As the evening had waned, so had my romantic interest in Steven. I yearned to return to the Ortega Street parking garage, thank him for a lovely time, get into my car, wave good-bye, and put the pedal to the metal.

When we walked from the wharf to the parking garage, Steven asked if I would give him a ride to his car, parked a mere three blocks away. I was wary of positioning myself within kissing-range of Steven; but I responded, "Of course I'll give you a ride," because I didn't want to appear rude. On the spot, I devised a haphazard plan to avoid Steven's kiss.

As I backed out of the white-lined slot and pulled beside the parking kiosk to pay the attendant, I accosted Steven with a deluge of deliberate hyperactivity. I became cartoon-animated and over-the-top bubbly. I hoped my manic behavior would persuade Steven to regard me as simply his fun-buddy and gal-pal. I hoped he'd view me as the furthest thing from kissable. Jeez, when had I morphed into such a prude?

I usually exited the garage by making a right turn onto Ortega Street and driving two blocks to Santa Barbara Street. There, I'd turn left and travel from downtown on a street invariably free of congestion. With Steven on board, my emergency tactic for kiss avoidance necessitated I forgo tranquil pathways of unwanted intimacy. I opted to drive my date to his car along the predictably crowded State Street.

I turned my car left onto Ortega Street, drove fifty feet, and then turned right onto State.

Like a menacing orca from the deep, a black and white police cruiser suddenly materialized behind my dolphin-esque vehicle. The squad car's rotating lights signaled me to pull over. I'm a good citizen. I obey the law. I pulled over.

I turned to Steven. "What did I do?"

Steven shrugged his shoulders. "I don't know."

I lowered my window and came face-to-torso with a bald, burly policeman of about fifty. "Hello, Officer, what did I do wrong?"

"You turned left out of the parking garage."

I motioned toward Steven and responded, "Well, Officer, he and I are on our first date, and we were engaged in animated conversation. I didn't notice any signs that instructed me not to turn left."

That's what I actually said to the cop. What I'd *wanted* to say was the truth—"*Officer, this man I'm with is a reeeally nice person, but in spite of his niceness, I've found myself faced with a dilemma. I'm pretty sure he was planning to kiss me, but I didn't want that to happen. I tried to create a distraction to discourage him from delivering on that kiss. It's uncertain whether I distracted him, but I definitely distracted myself. In fact, I was so distracted that I turned left from the parking garage instead of turning right like I always do. In hindsight, I've realized I should have done one of two things. I should've woman-upped and leveled with my date, or flat out kissed him and got it over with. And of course, I should have turned right.*"

"The signs that indicate no left turn are clearly visible," said the cop. "Have you had anything to drink tonight?"

"Yes, I had one glass of chardonnay with dinner."

"Where'd you eat dinner and what did you order?"

What an odd question. But maybe Officer Burly was looking for a recommendation—somewhere nice to take the missus.

"We ate at Killer Shrimp. It was tasty. We had shrimp in a savory broth, accompanied by fresh bread that we dipped into the broth. I don't usually eat bread, but the broth was much too spicy without it."

"How long ago did you eat?"

Hmm. What was this guy getting at?

"It's been at least two hours. After dinner we walked down to the wharf and sat to talk."

"Do you know what time it is now?"

"I don't know, maybe eleven? I wasn't keeping track."

"It's nearly midnight," said Officer Burly.

At that moment I sensed the tide had turned against me. Evidently, underestimating the time was against the law. The policeman at my window requested my driver's license.

"Would you mind stepping out of the car?"

"Okay," I said. *This is ridiculous!*

I got out of my car and stood on the red brick sidewalk. I noticed the burly officer was not alone; a woman cop of about forty stood nearby. Her complexion was olive. She wore her dark hair slicked back in a severe bun. She did not smile. In fact, her face was devoid of emotion, though perhaps that was not altogether true. Her face showed a trace of impatient condemnation. The pair's moodiness was contagious. My smile had faded too.

"You're gonna have to take a Breathalyzer test," said the officer.

I felt nauseous. The mere mention of the term "Breathalyzer test" made the shrimp in my belly threaten to revolt. Prior to the night I was stopped by police, I had never been in a situation where I was called upon to estimate my own blood alcohol level based on the amount of wine I'd ingested and the amount of time that had passed. I didn't understand how any of that worked.

"I'll need to think about it," I said. "Couldn't you ticket me for making a wrong turn, and let me go home?"

"No, I can't do that. You can either take a Breathalyzer test or we can drive you to county jail where you can take a blood test."

Adrenaline coursed through my system. My stomach churned. If my gut persisted with its nervous unrest, I'd be compelled to barf into a sidewalk planter of drought-tolerant plants.

"If I decided to go to county jail for the blood test, what would happen to my car?"

"We would have it towed."

"Couldn't my date drive my car to a safe place and park it on the street until morning?"

"No, he cannot do that."

Clearly, it wasn't just me who was in a bind, and it wasn't just me who was scrutinized. By association, Steven and my car had come under the cop's jurisdiction too. My anxiety subsided a bit, replaced by stubbornness. When I'm bullied, I don't give an inch.

"Well," I said to Officer Burly, "I feel like you're pressuring me to take a Breathalyzer test, but I need to be sure I'm making a good decision for myself. I've never been in this type of predicament. I really don't know what I should do." I looked to him for an expert's guidance, but I should have known better. Officer Burly wasn't big on doling out professional advice.

He pointed to the recessed entry of a dog-eared shop called Moon River, although you'll find no identifying sign out front. The place is commonly known by its address: 708 State Street.

"Step over there," he said. "I'm going to put you through a series of tests."

"Okay, sure." In my mind, I rolled my eyes. It must've been a slow night on patrol.

"Stand still, put your feet together, hands flat against your sides, and close your eyes."

I did so. I felt myself sway ever so slightly as I adjusted to my new position. I was a mighty oak whose leaves stirred undetected in a summer breeze. Barely a motion, but I knew I was damned. I have always been a bad balancer.

Next, Officer Burly had me count one to four, then backwards from four to one. I touched my thumb to each finger as I counted. I performed this task fluidly, and I didn't mess up once. Like a preschooler who'd mastered the skill of communicating his age by holding up the appropriate number of digits, I was proud of my dexterous finger-to-finger accomplishment. I felt a tad smug.

Then he instructed me to place my fists directly under my jaw, hold them there, and follow the beam of his small flashlight. My heart was beating rapidly. This man was not my ally. He would cut me no slack. In fact, I sensed we'd entered into some kind of twisted competition. Officer Burly *wanted* me to fail. I wanted to spare the drought-tolerant plants and barf on his shoes instead.

Following the flashlight test, Officer Burly instructed me to stand with my feet together. He told me to lift my left foot out in front of me and balance on my right. By that time I had stood on the sidewalk for at least thirty minutes. The night's chill caused me to shiver.

"Honestly, Officer, I've always been a bad balancer. Especially when I'm nervous. And I'm very nervous right now because you're not being nice, and I find you intimidating. I am nervous and I am cold. I'm shaking all over. There's no way I can successfully balance on one foot. I don't even want to try because you'll think my poor balance proves I'm drunk."

"Oh, so you think I'm intimidating, do you?"

"Yes, Officer, I do."

Officer Burly asked me how much extended education I'd had. Another peculiar question.

"Two years at Santa Barbara City College."

I was embarrassed to disclose this information. I feared Officer Burly would judge me for not acquiring a four-year college degree. I often judged myself for that very thing. If I was guilty of nothing else that night, I was certainly guilty of not furthering my education.

As it turned out, Officer Burly had inquired about my level of education because the next test was writing the alphabet in its entirety. He handed me a tiny spiral notepad and instructed me to write my ABCs. He told me when I finished I was to sign my name at the bottom of the page. Fortunately, my two otherwise aimless years at SBCC had included mastering the English alphabet.

I penciled my ABCs with confidence, carefully forming each letter in an uppercase block. I was tempted to showboat my skills by jotting down both uppercase letters and their lowercase equivalents, but I didn't want to risk provoking Officer Burly's ire. As I moved from letter J to K, I glanced at my car—headlights blazing—like a beacon of hope. Steven remained in the passenger seat, waiting, I supposed, for some indication of what he should do.

As I finished with my twenty-six letters arranged neatly in rows, a twenty-something man ran up to Officer Burly. Sweat dampened his lush hairline. The young man had sprinted two blocks from Joe's Cafe, where he'd been hanging out front with friends. He said he'd witnessed a man approach a woman, hit her in the stomach with a pole, and then flee.

Unmoved by the tale, Officer Burly told the man he was busy. He said he would radio another police officer to deal with the pole-hitting offense. Understandably, Officer Burly had more pressing matters. For instance, he had yet to review my ABCs. Then he needed to make sure I'd remembered to sign my name in cursive. My city's tax dollars hard at work.

"How did I do, Officer?"

"Not good."

My confidence was a sailboat dashed upon a rocky shore.

"What do you mean? Which test did I flunk?"

"The whole enchilada."

"I'm a writer! Certainly I passed my ABCs!"

"Yeah, you passed that one."

"What did I flunk then?"

"You swayed, you slurred your speech, your eyes didn't follow my flashlight, and you couldn't balance on one foot."

My brow furrowed, my jaw dropped. My mouth hung slack in astonishment and disbelief.

"Are you ready to take the Breathalyzer?"

"I just don't know what I should do. My son is waiting for me at home."

"If you don't make up your mind I'll have to handcuff you."

This man and I were at a standoff. He expected I'd buckle. I didn't want to award him the satisfaction.

"I cannot tell you your job, Officer."

Prior to that night, should anyone have asked me what police handcuffs were made of, I would have answered, "Steel." Standing on the sidewalk with Officer Burly, I'd come to understand handcuffs were forged from unbridled ego and the desire of one human to control another.

"Put your hands behind your back, palms together," said Officer Burly.

"Just like you're praying," piped in the long silent woman cop.

I wasn't the praying type, even in a pinch. Every time I'd petition the heavens I would hear God's voice reminding me I was sufficiently equipped with all I needed. I found it ironic that a woman (me) who no longer put her hands together in prayer, had been instructed to adopt such a position, albeit backwards, and dictated by armed officers of the law.

Officer Burly tightened my restraints, escorted me to the edge of the red curb, opened the rear door, and sat me down inside the squad car. Before the door to my wheeled cell was shut, I saw Steven emerge from my car, and step onto the curb. Though I'd noticed him there, his presence conjured neither curiosity nor hope.

Steven asked the female cop if he could talk with me. He wanted to advise me to take the Breathalyzer. He wanted to assure me I would have no problem passing since I'd had only one glass of wine with dinner three hours before. The cop said Steven wasn't allowed to talk to me. She told him I hadn't cooperated. She asked to see his driver's license and wrote something down. Steven's request on my behalf had made no impact. She ordered him to leave the scene. I was alone.

Officer Burly shut the back door of the police car. My anxiety skyrocketed. I was trapped, I was bound. I was purseless, dateless, and defenseless. I'd been buried alive. Any fate was preferable to sitting entombed in Officer Burly's squad car. The time had come for me to cry uncle for a crime I did not commit. I turned my body slightly in the seat and raised my cuffed wrists to the passenger window. I knocked twice on the window with my right elbow, paused, and then knocked again. I knew if he didn't open the door soon—if I wasn't able to feel the cool air rush in and around me—I might succumb to panic.

He opened the door. "Officer, I will take the Breathalyzer test!"

He said I would be required to blow into the Breathalyzer two separate times to ensure a correct reading. I did so. I resolved to accept whatever would come. Officer Burly stepped from my field of vision for several minutes, and then returned. He informed me I had passed. A warm wave of relief spread from the top of my head to my feet. I felt tears.

"See, I told you I couldn't stand steady on one foot because I was a bad balancer!"

"Most people who say that do so because they're too intoxicated to balance."

I never did ask Officer Burly what my blood alcohol level had registered. By that time I was reluctant to address him with anything he might interpret as confrontational. I just wanted him to take the cuffs off. I understood why an innocent defendant would agree to a plea bargain if the evidence was against him.

I hugged Officer Burly. It's odd that a beat dog will lick his master's hand. I inquired of my date's whereabouts. The woman cop said that Steven had left. I would never see him again.

Gratefully, I slumped into the driver's seat of my compact car, aware of how roomy it felt. I turned the key in the ignition. Nothing. The engine would not start. Evidently my headlights' bright "beacon of hope" had depleted the battery. I climbed from my sanctuary and approached my foe.

"Excuse me, Officer, one more thing. My car won't start."

"My car doesn't have jumper cables. I'll call in another squad car."

His countenance had lightened. A glimmer of mirth showed in his eyes and around his mouth. Now that I had proven my innocence, Officer Burly couldn't do enough to help.

A second police car arrived and parked its front bumper to face the raised hood of my car. I had two police cars and four members of law enforcement focused on my lil' crime-bedeviled self.

Riddle: How many cops does it take to jump-start a car?

Answer: Too many.

Another worthwhile use of taxpayer money.

Officer Burly never did issue me a ticket for exiting the Ortega Street parking garage in the wrong direction. Since then, I've wondered why.

Had Officer Burly realized he'd allowed a harmless incident to escalate to the absurd? Was his failure to ticket me a secret apology, perhaps his own personal show of remorse? If he had ticketed me after what he'd put me through, was he worried I'd contest the fine, and while I was at it, snitch? Had a ticket for my illicit exit never been Officer Burly's main objective? When he'd pulled me over, was he focused on a bigger score? Was he hoping—aspiring, even—to nail me for a DUI? Or, in the end, had Officer Burly's yen for hot cocoa and an apple fritter simply caused him to forget about the ticket?

There is at least one other explanation—an alternative narrative—to why I was not ticketed. It is a story I've only recently come to consider.

Earlier that evening, before my hands were positioned in vice versa prayer, and my wrists shackled—perhaps at the same time Steven and I sat talking on Stearns Wharf—the universe began to conjure magic that would soon intervene on my behalf. It's conceivable that, in the grand scheme of things, it was Officer Burly who stepped in as the fortuitous answer to my unuttered plea. Perhaps the powers-that-be saw fit to appoint *him* as the facilitator of my original objective: to avoid Steven's kiss. It's possible that Officer Burly was not my foe, but the opposite: my guardian angel. Beneath the tough-guy persona, it's likely he'd only had my best interest at heart. But, of course, I'll never know that for sure.

Cupid Gone Postal

I STOOD WITH ERIC IN THE SAND-SWEPT PARKING LOT at Hendry's Beach. I thought we were simply saying good-bye—and we were—but it was good-bye in the strictest sense of the word.

"Rebecca, thank you for taking a walk on the beach with me. I've enjoyed your company. You're a very nice person, but I think we should remain friends."

Friends. The f-word.

I was stunned; transfixed with disbelief. Whoa, wait a minute! *I'm* the one who's supposed to be the heartbreaker here! Rarely am I tongue-tied, but shock had stifled me. Before our date, I had made conscious concessions for this man—he was sort of goofy looking. I had lowered my standards and shelved my preferences. I had restructured my idealized list of "must-haves" to give an average guy like Eric a chance. I'd been prepared for the likelihood he would kiss me, but I hadn't considered that Eric would diss me.

I've been at the dating game long enough to realize what Eric's parting words had *really* meant— *"Rebecca, you're just not doing it for me. I can do much better than you."* That is the ego-wrenching reality about getting dumped. What the "dumper's" words mean is this: he thinks—*knows*—he would be settling for less should he decide to settle for you.

I could have returned his blow with one of my own, leveling both barrels at him—"*Eric, before you drive off in your BMW with surf racks—though you've confessed you don't surf—there's something I need to tell you. It appears you've overlooked a patch of whiskers while shaving this morning. And last week, when we met for tea? Well, you overlooked your whisker-patch that time too.*"

Determined I not expose my psyche's Achilles' heel, I bent to brush a fine layer of sand from where it clung to the instep of my left foot. My lower back—where I retain tension—absorbed the sun's therapeutic rays. I straightened. I gazed at the ocean, and commented on the pretty beach. And then I thanked him. For what? The pretty beach? For dumping me?

Eric and I had been introduced through eHarmony. I had long avoided subscribing to eHarmony because the site's system of matchmaking reminded me of vacationing aboard a cruise ship. On ship, one is hemmed in. The majority of one's stay is highly orchestrated, with set meal times, activity schedules, and stopovers in predetermined ports. A cruise is too restrictive for my taste—likewise, eHarmony. But one day, I decided to rock the boat. Although I remained doubtful, I resolved to give eHarmony a try.

The site's powers-that-be determined my male matches. If I like a man they've chosen, I'm encouraged to select five questions to send him via the site. If he is interested in me, he will answer my five questions, and email me five questions in return. Next comes a checklist of relationship "deal-breakers." I'm instructed to choose from a directory of character traits that would signal a swift demise to my relationship with a man: lying, cheating, bigotry, a toupee, cats. Subsequently, I forward my list to my potential match and he selects his relationship deal-breakers too.

Personally, this elaborate dance routine strikes me as over-complicated. Either a fellow subscriber will find me attractive or not. I don't think a set of arbitrary questions or checklists will translate to a more successful match. A true love match is made face-to-face, not upon a computer screen. When I spotted fifty-eight-year-old Eric's eHarmony profile, I cut to the chase, bypassed all questions and checklists, and emailed him directly.

In his return email, Eric asked if he could call me. We spoke on the phone, and later that week met for tea at Handlebar: a coffeehouse near El Cuartel, Santa Barbara's oldest residence. My initial attraction to Eric was minimal. Thin body. Thin hair. Nervous. Crest Whitestrips needed. As we stood at the counter to order our tea, I was momentarily distracted by a small thatch of gray whiskers that sprouted between Eric's left earlobe and jawline.

Eric and I took our mugs of peppermint tea to a small outside table where we sat and shared a relaxed exchange. He told me about his job, and we chatted about our kids. Eric peppered our conversation with his cynical sense of humor. His grin was disarming in a Dennis Quaid kind of way. As our time together drew to an end, I supposed there was a glimmer of mutual chemistry to build on.

As we stood to leave, my sweater became ensnared on a patio chair. I chuckled as I freed myself. Eric and I walked to the corner of Canon Perdido and Santa Barbara Street, where the light to cross was green. Eric shook my hand. "It was nice to meet you, Rebecca."

Was. He'd used the past tense. Already, Eric and I were history. If anybody had approached me then to inquire how our first date had gone, I would've said it had gone south. Eric did not mention wanting to see me again, so I assumed he didn't.

On my drive home I thought about Eric's whisker patch, his smile, and his mildly sarcastic wit. I'd liked him, yes, but my intuition signaled he might be the type of guy who'd mumble insults under his breath. It had become my habit to dismiss a man as unsuitable to offset my own disappointment. I made up my mind that Eric's sarcastic wit and his crop of overlooked whiskers constituted a dealbreaker. I wondered if eHarmony had *those* on their oh-so-discerning lists.

Apparently, however, Eric came to his senses. Days later, he called to arrange our beach walk. We agreed to meet at the wooden steps at one o'clock. Although Eric looked more attractive than he had at tea and was otherwise clean-shaven, his odd thatch remained. Eric was barefoot, so I kicked off my flip-flops for our walk. Unbeknownst to me, it would become the walk that would seal our doomed romantic fate. What had gone wrong?

I don't know. Perhaps I wasn't the only one who was distracted by insignificant flaws. Maybe Eric had not liked my freckles, or my two tattoos, or my funky sun hat, or my laugh. Maybe he didn't think I was pretty enough, or smart enough, or sarcastic enough. It could have been any or all of the above. Or something else entirely. I have a history of discrediting men for unjustifiable reasons. Like cupid gone postal, I've broken my share of hearts. When Eric dumped me, I had it coming.

Is it wise for us to wait indefinitely for our perfect match? Is it not prudent to accept the possibility that if we wait too long we may never discover our life's mate? Are we routinely bypassing individuals who may be good matches for us because we have too soon determined they do not meet our strict criteria? Do we possess the humility to admit that we may not have the wherewithal to recognize who the best match for us might be?

Online dating sites have perpetuated the myth that one's ideal romantic partner is but a profile away. With so many choices, it's tempting to discredit viable matches prematurely. Maybe we online daters should curtail our endless search for nonexistent perfection, embrace our own limitations, and take our chances with an imperfect individual who is *perfect enough*. I had thought Eric a "perfect enough" prospect, although he was not my fanciful ideal. Prior to our first date, I had resolved to cut the guy some slack and refrain from being overly judgmental, yet it was his judgment of me that prevailed. Perhaps love will happen when it happens—without undue strife or excessive compromise. About this, I am no expert. About this, I remain unsure.

Tomorrow I will log on to eHarmony, as imperfect as it may be. I will consider the men selected for me, and I will determine whether I am interested enough to forward any of them my five arbitrary questions. After all, I have a six-month subscription. I think I'm entitled to some degree of dating success for my money. I've paid my dues.

Cocky Old Penises

THREE WEEKS SHY OF MY FIFTY-SEVENTH, I got tattooed in Texas. My birthday tat eclipsed a preexisting one, "Liberty," a rebellious "I'm free!" statement I chose when I exited my marriage nine years before. The cover-up was a butterfly, a gentler black-and-blue design more suitable to a wiser, and calmer, middle-aged woman's upper left arm.

According to the tattoo studio's elaborately inked employee—who sported one-inch ear gauges—company policy required he accept cash only. Also mandated by law, I had to present my California driver's license. I handed over both. He laid my four twenty-dollar bills atop the Windexed counter, bent his head to the task at hand, and studied my laminated ID. After a moment he looked up.

"How old are you?"

Aww shit. Please God, not this . . .

"Are you inquiring so you can make fun of me?"

"No. I don't believe the birth date on your license."

I must've misunderstood. The low buzz of electric needles could

be heard coming from behind a pirate flag that doubled as a doorway curtain.

"You're kidding, right? How old did you think I was?"

I held my breath—waiting.

"Thirty-five."

Exhale.

"Can I give you a hug, please?"

He came around to my side of the counter and we embraced in a heartfelt hug. I assume it was more heartfelt on my end than on his, but he was kind enough to indulge me. At that moment, I would have given him more than a hug. I could've kissed him—and thrown in a courtesy blowjob. Afterwards, we'd get matching tattoos.

I have to face it. As a middle-aged woman, I do not receive the amount of male attention I once did. Should a misguided individual in "real life" mistake me as younger, I'm stunned by disbelief because my online experience has not been equally gracious. Internet dating sites cultivate the myth that men my age, or older—those with saggy jowls and comb-overs—can select, order, and bag whichever woman they desire—the younger the better—as if she were a new putter, cozy shearling seat covers, or a stainless steel barbecue for their patio. It appears that a number of men who subscribe to Match.com are focused on a woman's age, to the exclusion of her talents, intelligence, or beauty. The gross age prejudice I've encountered among middle-aged men is the very reason I'll remain eternally grateful to a certain young Texan.

Over the years I've read thousands of men's online dating profiles, and I've noticed a trend. A fair number of men my age or older seek *only* younger women. I too am open to dating younger, and I've done so, yet I'm also eager to date men in my age demographic that have maintained an active lifestyle. To me, a man's age is not as important as his good health, positive energy, and youthful appearance. Do I think it possible that men could evolve to adopt my point of view? Of course; if I gave them a two-by-four upside the head.

When an individual purchases a subscription to Match.com, they are required to complete a personal questionnaire that is posted for public viewing on the Match.com site. Members of the site have access to other members' information regarding marital status, height/weight/body type, eye/hair color, ethnicity, religious/political affiliation, number of children, tobacco and alcohol habits, and the age they'd prefer to date. A subscriber can post any age range they're open to. My current Match.com profile states that I will consider men as young as forty-nine, and as old as sixty-five.

One afternoon I logged on to my Match.com account with the intention of conducting my own sociological "study." My objective was to focus on the maximum-age cap that men and women had selected for their profiles. I was curious if my observations of males' age biases could be supported. I scrolled through the first two hundred profiles posted by male subscribers ages 45–65, who lived within twenty-five miles of my zip code. I wanted to see how many men had set the maximum age they would date as younger than themselves, and how many men were willing to date women five to ten years older than themselves. I repeated the process with the opposite sex. The results of my poll were more disheartening than I'd anticipated.

Of the two hundred men I reviewed, 56 percent specified they would date women their age or older. Of those, 39.5 percent of the men placed their maximum age cap at up to four years older than themselves, while 12 percent of the men placed their maximum age cap at five to nine years older. Only 4.5 percent of the men placed

their maximum age cap at over ten years older than themselves. One accommodating forty-seven-year-old man claimed he'd date women ages 35–100. Would he really?

On the flip side, 44 percent of the two hundred men I reviewed live in fantasyland. These were the gentlemen who placed their maximum age cap at younger than themselves. My study showed that 23.5 percent placed their maximum age cap at one to four years younger, and 16 percent placed their maximum age cap at five-plus years younger than themselves. The most audacious of all, 4.5 percent placed their *maximum* age cap at ten-plus years *younger* than themselves. A never-married fifty-three-year-old man specified women 27–33. He said he wanted to father children before it was "too late." Another man posted: *Wealthy 46-year-old developer seeks classy girl, age 18–35, for long-term relationship.* What enterprising lass would bypass such a bargain? When her old man is pushing up daisies, she'll still be young enough to enjoy a "long-term relationship"—with his money.

The women, on the other hand? Astonishingly different. While 1.5 percent of the two hundred women I reviewed placed their maximum age cap at equal to their own age, a whopping 97 percent specified they would date men older than themselves. In the geriatric-seeking sect, 26.5 percent placed their maximum age cap at up to four years older, while 41.5 percent placed their maximum age cap at five to nine years their senior. A significant number—29 percent—placed their maximum age cap at ten-plus years older than themselves. A mere three women—1.5 percent—placed their maximum age cap at *younger* than themselves.

My survey determined that 56 percent of the men I reviewed on Match.com were open to dating a woman whose age equaled or exceeded their own. Good news, right? Kind of. Until one considers that 98.5 percent of all women I reviewed were open to dating a man their age or older. It's sobering to realize that 44 percent of the men I reviewed specified they would date *only* younger women, compared to the 1.5 percent of the women who specified they'd date only younger men.

Have women on Match.com been pressed to become more flexible with the age of the men they'd date because men are generally less flexible with the age of women they'd consider dating? The results of my study suggest that as a woman ages, she will find it more difficult to secure dates from Match.com. As a woman ages, she will be pressed to date ever-older men. Although 97 percent of the women I reviewed were already open to this, women tend to outlive men. In time, an aging woman's mature suitors will dwindle due to natural mortality rates.

I've heard it said that men believe they possess more allure than is merited, while women believe they possess less. A woman will hold herself accountable for nature's inevitable gifts of cellulite and gray hair, whereas a pudgy balding man will look in the mirror and see himself as he'd looked in high school. My survey seems to support this. Apparently, a fair number of codgers believe they still have what it takes to lasso a filly. Evan wrote: *Though I'm flattered by the emails I've received from women older than 45, please check my age preference. If you are over, pass me up. I'm not a typical 52-year-old ;-)* Should you encounter a situation like this, take narcissistic Evan's advice—pass him up. On second thought, take it one step further. Delete his profile in the name of vermin eradication.

I do understand the appeal of an older man who offers financial comfort and worldliness to a younger woman, but what does an old hippie with scraggly facial hair and broken teeth offer? Male bravado knows no limits! Yet, to belabor the absurdity of men's preferences does nothing to alter men's preferences.

I suppose women have the option to lie about their age if they think they can pull it off, and who among us would admit we couldn't succeed at such a prank? I've listened in as a respected dating coach encouraged middle-aged women to fabricate their age online as a way "to get their foot in the door" and expose themselves to men who ordinarily date younger. While I acknowledge the coach's point, I disagree. Integrity should remain a woman's bottom line. Living in truth is more valuable than landing a man. Each woman must draw her own personal line in the sand that represents her dating standards. Two years ago, I vowed to never again have casual sex with an unsheathed or commitment-shy penis. My resolution joined a long-standing one: I don't lie about my age.

I'm coming to realize I can kick and scream my way into my elder years, or I can opt to tread peacefully. I aspire to choose a serene journey, yet the society in which I reside celebrates—*worships*—youth. If each woman were to receive the guarantee that she would transition into midlife securely and lovingly tethered to a romantic partner who bolstered her confidence, perhaps she would never require a stranger's reassurance that she is still desirable. I've learned firsthand: *the ego doesn't age.* Whenever suitable men in my age demographic pass me by to pursue more youthful options, the rejection delivers a profound sting.

Prior to turning fifty, I didn't believe it possible that time would search me out, creep up from behind, and slowly have its way with my face, my body, and my identity. My reluctance to accept the aging process, and my incomprehension as to how such a thing could happen to *me*, has slowly, tentatively, eased into acceptance, wonder, and a state of gratefulness that I've been gifted with the privilege to grow up, and to grow old. What a blessing it would be to have a suitable man beside me.

Pop! Goes the Weasel

I HADN'T SLEPT WELL. In the morning I drove Shoreline Drive to La Playa Stadium. I parked across the street at Leadbetter Beach. Lady Luck had saved me a spot in front of the café, where parking is free for ninety minutes. I stepped from my car and donned my running shoes and cap. *Damn!* I'd forgotten an elastic band for my hair. That small detail triggered undue anxiety. Unruly long hair and athletic caps don't mix—unless we're talking Swamp People fashion.

A distant train horn, much too loud and much too urgent, overfilled the space around my head. I didn't wait for the green light. I jaywalked across Shoreline Drive and entered the junior college's football stadium. I'd been looking forward to climbing the steep concrete steps that rise above the track and field. Exercise remedies stress. I had a lot on my mind.

As I reached the lofty eighty-fourth step, I happened upon him doing push-ups on the concrete terrace where the three press boxes are located. His sculpted body looked like it had been carved from flawless black marble at the hand of Michelangelo. He stood and smiled. He was young. I guessed him to be no more than thirty.

"You look great," I said. It has never been my practice to withhold compliments. If I'm thinking good thoughts—well-intentioned thoughts—why not share them? It's the way I roll.

"Thank you. Are you single?" He had an accent I couldn't place. Maybe Jamaican.

His question had surprised me. I'd immediately recognized he was too young—too beautiful—to be showing me special consideration.

I looked away from him. I scanned the horizon and took in the panoramic view of the harbor. Colorful flags stationed along the length of the breakwater were alive in the wind, proclaiming goodwill to land dwellers and seafarers alike. Waves pounded the neighboring beach with a startling intensity that gave rise to a foggy mist that rolled across the street and settled on the football field. The wind carried the scents of sunbaked kelp and Coppertone.

I broke free of nature's spell and refocused my attention on the ebony man.

"Yes, I'm single," I said.

"My name is Zuri. Do you want to date me?"

I laughed. "You don't miss a beat, do you?"

"I try not to miss anything. Would you like to go to tea?"

The night before, I had broken it off with a guy I really liked, a hunk of a man who'd melted my butter into a golden liquid ideal for dipping succulent lobster. His name was Garrett. From the time of our first phone conversation, he had held the monopoly on my attention.

"Hey darlin'! Whatcha doin' today?" Garrett had called me darlin'. I liked him right away.

"I'm writing, hanging with my son, and later, at four, I have a wine date."

"That's ironic! I'm on my way to a surf date with a lady. Can I call you after?"

"Sure. Call me if you want to. Have fun on your date!" I was cucumber cool.

My phone rang at 2:30. It was Garrett. "Hey darlin'!"

"Cowabunga!" I said. Garrett laughed. Make a man laugh, and you've set the bait for love.

"I'm just checking in. My date was an awesome surfer, as good, if not better, than me. She caught some pretty amazing waves. I was impressed."

"So, were there sparks?"

"No. To tell you the truth, I found myself thinking of you."

I laughed. He had baited me too.

Garrett was an artist, a surfer, and a skater: the telltale description of a free spirit. Match.com had determined us compatible, and I'd been pleased with the pairing. I emailed him something silly like—*art rocks!*

I hadn't expected Garrett to message me back. He was five years younger than me, and if I was to trust the photos he'd posted online, Garrett was a hottie. To my surprise, he did email me, and he requested my number to boot. I was reluctant.

Nine years earlier, and fresh out of my seventeen-year marriage, I had dated a man who was an artist, skater, stoner, and free spirit. Things hadn't fared well, although I'd given him plenty of breathing room. For a time, he tried to be a boyfriend to me, but he'd neither the guts nor the glue to make it stick. After a while, he met a younger woman who forfeited her opportunity to become a wife and a mother in order to live with a free spirit of a man, tend his children, and hold together the frayed ends of his ramshackle life.

When a man is a free spirit, he lives life on his terms. He may harbor narcissistic tendencies when it comes to bending his lifestyle to fit alongside another's. A free spirit is an opportunist, waiting for situations to arise that will benefit him, then heading off in another direction whenever it suits his fancy. A free spirit is fun to be around. They are the embodiment of spontaneous adventure, and should somebody step up to fund it, all the better. Working a consistent job cramps their creativity as well as their compulsion for freedom. I understand some of what drives a free spirit. To choose exactly how I live my life has always been paramount to my happiness. I resist being hemmed in by the dictates of society. A nine-to-five job would incite major depression. I desire to live a simple, flexible existence that allows me to remain receptive to new possibilities. I am a bit of a free spirit myself.

Although I had returned an upbeat response to Garrett's initial email, I'd ignored his request that I leave my number. He sent me this reply: *I hope we'll have an opportunity to meet. If not, may your search bring you everything you desire.* How could I refuse this man? After all, my free-spirited ex-boyfriend's behavior had nothing to do with this new guy, right? I emailed Garrett my phone number. Seven minutes later we were having our first conversation. That day he called three times; once, to inquire how my afternoon wine date had gone.

We'd been aware of each other's existence for only forty-eight hours. During that short period Garrett called six times. Once, we talked from 9:00 p.m. until he fell asleep—still talking—at midnight. He reminded me of a flaming comet. Unstoppable. I was worried about burnout. I cautioned Garrett to slow down, take his time, get to know me, and be my friend.

"Well, darlin', I want us to be more than friends. Every time we talk, I get a bigger crush on you. Can I call you tonight?"

Two and a half days following our first phone chat I prepared to meet Garrett for wine in Santa Ynez Valley: a location equidistant from where we each lived. I took extra time with my makeup, my hair, my dress. I have been on so many first dates that anxiety beforehand had become an anomaly, but I was nervous about my date with Garrett. He seemed too good to be true.

Before I stepped through the door of the Los Olivos restaurant where we had agreed to meet, I paused to gather myself. My heart beat rapidly. Tiny beads of perspiration formed on my nose. I blotted my nose with a tissue, stuffed it into my coat pocket, and pulled open the door.

Inside the Petros entry stood my date—a gorgeous specimen of a man—casually dressed in a short-sleeved cotton button-down shirt, loose-fitting khakis, and black Converse. Both of his forearms were richly tattooed.

"What took you so long?" Garrett teased. "I've been waiting forty-five minutes." He'd known I would be there at six. I walked in just as the town's bells chimed. Garrett had arrived early to guarantee I wouldn't be left waiting.

We remained in the restaurant's rustic-chic lounge where we sat in two plush upholstered chairs positioned on either side of a polished burl-wood table. Garrett said he wasn't much of a wine drinker, so I suggested we order something light: a bottle of sauvignon blanc. Also appetizers: garlic lamb pizza and pita triangles with a creamy radish spread.

While we waited for our wine, Garrett and I flirted and exchanged casual chitchat. I leaned forward across the low table and met his unwavering gaze. "Garrett, you're too cute for me!"

My hunky date was six feet tall, broad shouldered, and well muscled, with chin-length blonde hair, a five-days' growth of gold and silver stubble, and gray-blue eyes.

"Awww . . . you're sweet, Rebecca, but you're talking nonsense. When you walked in the door, I thought, 'Oh my god!'"

Throughout my life, the complimentary statement "Oh my god!" had been reserved for my statuesque younger sister, who, at age nineteen, won the Miss Miller High Life bikini contest in an understated one-piece bathing suit. "Oh my god!" was something lavished upon my best friend who was crowned Homecoming Queen at both our high school and community college. To the best of my knowledge, "Oh my god!" was a phrase that'd never been aimed at me. Until Garrett.

"Why are you sitting way over there?" said Garrett. "Do you want to come and sit on my lap?"

Without hesitation, I sprang from my chair and plopped myself smack-dab on Garrett's lap. I positioned my face a breath from his. As he spoke, I stared at his beautiful mouth, the way the right side lifted more than the left when he smiled, the fine vertical lines in his lips, the white and strawberry-gold whiskers that I longed to brush my lips against, a cluster of tiny bubbles of saliva resting on his tongue, and the reflection of the room's soft light on his teeth. We kissed—softly, then firmly—multitudes of hot fervent exploratory ones. He'd tasted of fresh garlic and the sea. We were a flash fire that threatened to burn the place down.

Sitting together in our chair, Garrett confided that he hadn't wanted to marry his former wife, although he said he'd loved her. He said he didn't believe a marriage license was a necessity if two people were committed. I felt a sharp sting of disappointment. I have little patience for that type of reasoning, since I would like to be married again. Although he'd been divorced for as long as I, Garrett didn't appear a likely candidate for another trip down the aisle. It was doubtful I'd be the woman to change his mind.

He said he had treasured the experience of being a stay-at-home parent while his wife went off to work. He'd once retrieved his daughter from school on his skateboard—sitting on the deck with her as they'd cruised down the hill toward home. Now, with both kids grown, he welcomed his greater freedom.

"I told you I have a thirteen-year-old son at home, right?"

"Yes, you did. That would be a consideration," he said.

Most of the time he lived in his van, camping on a friend's secluded beach property north of Santa Barbara. When not at the beach, Garrett lived at another friend's house while he worked on the home's remodel. He said he contemplated a move to Hawaii.

Why had this man bothered to pursue me when his message was loud and clear? *I like you, Rebecca, but don't get too attached.* Garrett was a rolling stone—a drifter. Only his van stood between him and homelessness.

At closing time, we were the last guests remaining. Our waitress brought the bill. Garrett asked me if I minded going dutch. "Dutch" is a reasonable proposition when I am out to lunch with a girlfriend. The word is much less favorable coming from a man who'd just swabbed my mouth with his deliciously lusty tongue. My libido cooled by fifteen degrees.

"I'm not sure if I have enough money in my account to cover this," he said. "I have money due me, but it hasn't been deposited yet." The bill, including tip, was a hundred dollars.

"No problem, Garrett. Let me pay and you can pick up the tab next time." Developments like this are one of the reasons I prefer to keep the first date to a single glass of wine or a piping hot cup of tea. When an individual of my diminutive size drinks half a bottle of wine, said wine will transform itself into a potent serum of truth. The waitress returned to our table to collect my debit card. "Can I get you two anything else tonight?"

I said, "A room, perhaps? But no, forget it, I'd have to pay for that, too."

I had regretted my words as soon as they'd left my mouth. Like toothpaste squirted from the tube, my words could not be returned. They lay like a coil of chalky ooze in the bathroom sink. I turned to Garrett, held his face in my hands, and apologized.

"That was totally reactionary of me! I'm so sorry!"

And I was sorry. I was sorry for my hurtful words. I was also sorry Garrett didn't believe in marriage. I was sorry he lived in his van, or couch-surfed at his friend's house. I was sorry he planned to move to Hawaii, and I was sorry he had under a hundred dollars to his name. I was sorry that I'd met a hot, attentive, charismatic guy who was programmed to love his freedom more than he would ever love me.

Garrett said he'd had a wonderful time—the best first date ever. As we exited the restaurant, he suggested we continue kissing in my car. "No," I said. "That's enough for one night. Let's not rush things."

He emailed me the next day—Monday—to say he needed to restock his food supplies. Would I agree to meet him if he drove to Santa Barbara on Wednesday to shop? Would I grab dinner with him afterwards? I'd a foreboding feeling that to bank on Garrett for any sort of stability would be akin to trusting I could walk on clouds. But I liked him. I didn't want to say no. I said yes.

At 6:00 p.m., he stood waiting for me outside of Trader Joe's. As I climbed from my car, I spotted him there—tall and unaware of his appeal—leaning on a post in front of the automatic glass door. He wore white loose-fitting pants patterned with a thin-lined plaid, a body-hugging short-sleeved T-shirt, tennis shoes, a knit cap with a brim, and reading glasses. I smiled at his unique fashion sense. Quietly, I approached. "Hey, darlin'!" he said as he wrapped his arms around me.

The store's fluorescent lighting seemed overly bright. Shoppers swirled around us, floating, like ghosts in the ballroom at Disneyland's Haunted Mansion. Garrett and I walked the aisles. Beside him, I felt elation coupled with nausea. I knew from my experience, as well as from the cautionary advice of others, that the rush of intense physical attraction can throw one's better judgment off-kilter. I wanted us to be the exception, to have a dose of manic chemistry and also possess what it took for the long haul. We parked his cart in front of the bakery display to kiss. The stacks of apple pies, brownie bites, and carrot cupcakes were my witnesses. I'd gone bananas for the guy.

We traveled through the checkout and then rolled the stainless steel shopping cart out front.

"Hey, darlin', do you wanna go bowling? Zodo's is right down the street."

"Sure, but I wore flip-flops. I don't have socks."

"I have a pair in my van you can have."

Garrett stored his groceries in the van and grabbed his coat, as well as a pair of Tommy Hilfiger socks—"I just washed 'em, darlin'." He grasped my hand, and we walked the couple of blocks to the bowling alley. We sat glued together in a private booth and feasted on hamburgers, fries, and beer, while we waited for a lane to open up.

"I'm surprised you wanted to date me," I said. "Last week I turned fifty-seven."

"I don't care how old you are. I like you." I believed him.

Garrett paid for the beer and burgers. I paid for bowling. Knowledge of Garrett's finances had guilted me into it. My first game, I broke 100: a miracle.

Afterwards, we walked to a neighboring drugstore where Garrett purchased ice for his ice chest and a razor. He said he planned to be clean-shaven for our next date. In the cashier's presence, Garrett remarked that he'd like to see me in lingerie. I was aware I'd just kissed Garrett in the company of God and the carrot cupcakes, but *I* was no "cupcake." His personal comment in front of a stranger made me—us—appear smutty. I made light of my discomfort and joked off Garrett's comment.

The night had cooled. Garrett donned his coat. It resembled a curly black lamb jacket my grandmother had owned.

"Aren't you pimpin' it!" I teased.

"Yeah, I probably look gay."

"No, you look like a big cuddly bear." His unconventional garb was part of his charm.

"I thought you'd like to hug me in this."

I was flattered by Garrett's efforts to please me. If only he'd had a place of his own, a steady job, a smaller, less pervy vehicle. Wasn't it sort of creepy that he transported his bedroom along on every date? I wondered about the amount of action that had ensued in the back of his van.

"Rebecca, I've brought you presents. They're in my van."

"You did? That was nice of you! Is this a ploy to get me inside your van?"

"Do I need a ploy to do that?"

I felt Garrett was backing me into a corner where escape would be iffy at best. I was certain of my attraction to Garrett—that was a no-brainer—but I was wary of us becoming overly physical too soon.

Garrett unlocked the van's front passenger door and opened it. I peered in. On top of his vehicle's expansive dashboard, he'd assembled a miniature beach scene: white sand, shells, fragments of gray driftwood, a pink cocktail umbrella, and a hula girl figurine. Garrett's tiny landscape added an element of hippie charm to his old van, but I couldn't get past imagining the inevitable mess of all that loose sand. From his mini beach, Garrett plucked two lavender urchin skeletons—tiny ellipsoid UFOs—and two pale sand dollars—flying saucers. Of each pair, one shell was slightly larger than the other. All four treasures fit in the palm of his hand.

"I found them on my friend's beach. Their size is symbolic of us."

"They're perfect. Thank you."

"Come lay with me, Rebecca."

Garrett's old white cargo van was the type without many windows: Chevy? Dodge? Ford? I didn't know. It's always been my habit to pay little attention to unnecessary details. Instead, I willingly climbed into the belly of a great-white-shark-on-wheels to be with him. Garrett closed the door.

Behind the front bucket seats was open space. Six or seven men's shirts, their shoulders lined up neatly on metal hangers, hung from a rod mounted on the ceiling behind the driver's seat. Marine-blue indoor-outdoor carpet covered the floor. A foam pad, two layers thick to afford extra comfort, lay butted up against an interior wall beneath the hanging shirts. There was a bed pillow too, encased in white cotton fabric. I detected the residual odor of marijuana. As if he'd read my mind, Garrett slid open a tiny horizontal window to allow for ventilation. He took off his coat and tossed it on the passenger's seat, where it did not remain. Like an inky shadow, the coat slipped from its vinyl perch and fell to the floor. A cool gust entered the tiny window, stirring up a fine layer of dashboard sand. Gold silica rained upon the curly pelt—a sleeping lamb in a sandstorm.

Garrett lowered his body onto the makeshift mattress and rested his head on the pillow. I lay down next to him, tucked my head beneath his chin, and nuzzled into the warm pulse of his neck. Garrett's short whiskers felt soft—and then prickly—as my face rubbed against them. I closed my eyes. With a steady inhale, I filled my lungs with his healthy man-scent.

"Umm, you smell nice."

"Thank you, darlin'. Before our date, I showered with a jug of Sparkletts."

I laughed, and withdrew my head from its musky recess. Garrett kissed me as he unbuckled my belt, slipped his hand inside my jeans, and brought me to orgasm.

It must have been after 10:00 p.m. The Trader Joe's parking lot was quiet. I sat up. What was I thinking? And what the hell was I doing in the back of a cargo van with Peter Pan?

Garrett's penis had been set loose from the confinement of its owner's pants. If I hadn't come prepared with socks for bowling, what made Garrett think I'd come prepared with condoms for sex? The nursery rhyme "Pop! Goes the Weasel" played inside my head: *The monkey thought it all in fun, Pop! goes the weasel.* Monkey-me thought our date had been super fun. Why had Garrett's impatient weasel popped up and ruined everything?

"I want to be inside you."

"I don't have sex unless I'm in a committed relationship." I felt priggish, but resolute.

"We're not there yet, Rebecca."

"Yes, I know that. This is our second date."

"I've been out of a relationship for just three months," he said. "I think maybe I should date around, but I also want to find love. I'm just scared, I guess."

"I understand. That's why I don't want to get emotionally attached to you before you're ready. I'm really happy with my life and I want to keep it that way. I think I should go."

I'd broken our lusty spell. Garrett's weasel had lost its pop.

"Okay. Let me walk you to your car. Please email me when you get home."

When I arrived home, I sent Garrett an email.

I had the most awesome time with you tonight, Garrett! Every minute of it was great. I'm certain you know I'm not exaggerating. :-) I have been divorced for nine years. My last relationship was over two years ago and I'm ready to try my hand at love again. I appreciate your honesty about where you're at in your life. I'm more than a little bummed we're not in the same place. I like you so much, but I need to stay focused on what I'm ultimately seeking. I trust you will understand. Thank you for the beautiful shells. I placed them in my kitchen window so I can enjoy them often. You are the sweetest! ~Rebecca

Garrett replied that he understood—that he too needed to remain true to his direction. He said he was happy our paths had crossed. He said he felt love for me and my beautiful soul. He'd closed with Xs and Os.

That was it. I was relieved by the graciousness of his goodwill. And shocked. And wounded. He'd let me go so easily.

Everything had happened so rapidly. Garrett vanished from my life before I had time to make sense of it. Twelve hours later, I remained blanketed by confusion. At La Playa Stadium I met Zuri, who'd asked me to tea. If Garrett had stayed in the picture, I would not have gone with Zuri. I would have laughed jovially at his invitation—flattered—yet undeterred. And I would have said no: "*I appreciate your offer, but I already have someone who thinks I'm special—my cup runneth over.*"

The reality was, I had nobody special. I'd absolutely nothing to forfeit by going to tea with this young man. I had just lost what I'd thought I'd wanted. When one has already lost, what more can they lose?

I waited for him in front of Coffee Cat on Saturday at five. The hands of the courthouse clock informed me my date was ten minutes late. At 5:13 I spotted Zuri, half a block away. Even from that distance he was hard to miss.

Zuri's caramel-colored topsiders and ivory T-shirt were the only subtle pieces of his odd ensemble. Camouflage-patterned skinny jeans in khaki and green were rolled to midcalf, exposing his trim ankles and lean muscular legs. On top he wore the understated T-shirt beneath a dinner jacket sewn from material that appeared to be zebra hide. The strap of his black pleather shoulder bag crossed his chest diagonally, and the attached man-purse rested below his right hip. A chunky gold-link necklace hung to midchest, and two wide gold bracelets embedded with colorful stones encircled his left wrist. Zuri's short bleached dreadlocks were crowned with a ribbon of gilded laurel.

"Sorry I'm late. I was driving around, unsure which parking garage to use."

"That's okay," I said. It's my habit to accept apologies even when I don't mean it.

Zuri held open the door to Coffee Cat and I walked in. I had already been inside once before, at five o'clock, when I'd arrived on time.

"Wow, what an outfit!" I said. What I thought was: *Really? You'd dress like that? You look like a pimp!* What I'd *wanted* to do was leave. What I'd *wanted* to do was run down the sidewalk screaming at the absurdity of my life. But I didn't. Instead, I smiled. I hung in there. I stuck it out. "This is nothing like what I usually wear," said Zuri. "I've toned it down this afternoon."

Zuri paid for our cups of peppermint tea and we chose a booth. I was surprised at the sorry state of the upholstery. The padded seating looked like it had been salvaged from a junkyard pickup truck; a bench seat composed of worn patches was held together with gray duct tape. The wooden tabletop was etched by years of use and was probably teeming with bacteria. I was grateful I'd ordered boiling microbe-killing tea.

Zuri's smile was broad, a friendlier version of the Cheshire Cat. His teeth were large and white, yet not perfect. His front incisors were slightly misaligned, chipped at the inside, and unevenly pigmented, perhaps the result of a childhood illness. I soon learned Zuri had survived a civil war in his native Liberia. That he'd made it out alive was a miracle.

He asked me about my interests and how I spent my time. "My son, my writing, working out, going on bad dates," I said. He smiled. The Cheshire Cat at Coffee Cat. Zuri told me he'd asked me out because he had wanted something. His beguiling smile and the invitation to tea had been a calculated ploy. Zuri said he entertained hope I would hire him as my "companion," someone I'd take to dinner, or invite over to watch a movie. I wouldn't be his only client, he said. He had an established clientele of middle-aged women who paid him for his services. He said he was also for hire as a personal trainer, life coach, musician, composer, and exotic dancer, whose bachelorette party skills left nary a bride-to-be worthy of white on her wedding day. Zuri had pity for the poor saps who would never please their new wives the way he'd done. These men were only mortals, he said. He did not include himself among them.

Zuri reached his burnished hand into the musky mystery of his purse and brought forth a business card—the type with a magnetic backing—perfectly suited to the task of securing my son's seventh grade report card to the door of our refrigerator. He extended his zebra-cloaked arm across the table to hand me his card.

I studied it—a sepia-toned photo of Zuri—shirtless, exquisitely muscled, his hands tied to a sturdy wooden fence, crucifixion style. His bowed head was crowned with laurel.

He thinks he's Jesus!

I looked up to meet Zuri's gaze. "I'm a busy woman," I said. "I'm not bored with my life nor with my own company. I don't need to pay men to hang out with me." I wondered if my confidence would return to haunt me. I finished my tea.

I offered to walk Zuri to his car. He had a difficult time remembering where he had parked. Gauging from his high opinion of himself, as well as his flamboyant mode of dress, I had expected more from his vehicle—a Mercedes, BMW, or a pimpin' Cadillac to complement his attire. Instead, his car was a badly oxidized compact: Mazda? Toyota? Ford? I don't remember. I only remember that it had Texas plates. Zuri said he didn't own a car. He'd borrowed this jewel from his sister.

He asked me to stay in touch. "I will," I said. I always assure my dates I'll stay in touch. Even when I don't mean it.

I've arrived at the part of my story where it gets tricky for me. I'm compelled to consider how Garrett and Zuri's motives were similar, although to do so involves exposing my tender underbelly. I'm inclined to pigeonhole Zuri as arrogant, self-serving, and ostentatious. I'm tempted to demonize him: a gigolo who sells himself to vulnerable middle-aged women. I desire to hold a gentler view of Garrett: a well-intentioned free spirit who got carried away by passion. I want to gift my trampled ego some consolation. I want to believe his feelings for me were sincere. But I'm not certain this is the truth.

Garrett was a drifter who chose to live his life by the seat—and the crotch—of his pants. He was a fifty-two-year-old man who lived in his van, and he relied on the generosity of others to keep himself afloat. He pursued what served him in the short term. His life was evidence he'd not aspired to long-term investments. Zuri went after what benefited him in the short term as well, but perhaps, between the two, Zuri was most honest. He'd asked for what he'd wanted up front.

Both were physically beautiful men, nonconformists, with engaging smiles, buoyant personalities, and confident senses of style. It would be idiotic to assume I'd been the only woman with whom Garrett shared magnetic chemistry. Had he collected treasures at the shore with me in mind? Or, did he simply retrieve the shells from his dashboard display as a last-minute means to weaken my resolve? Had both men supposed I'd graciously provide them financial aid, or sex? And, did my trusting nature convince both Garrett and Zuri that I'd be an easy score?

I take full responsibility for succumbing to the charismatic pull of Garrett's body. I had been uncertain whether I'd still be capable of experiencing the intoxicating nausea of intense physical chemistry, yet at fifty-seven, the hormones of my twenty-five-year-old self made their welcomed comeback. I am grateful. Above all, I am grateful that various lessons over the years have taught me to trust my judgment in the moment, and not assume that what a man wants from me is more important than what I want for myself. I've learned to love me most. If I don't, nobody else will. I didn't know that at twenty-five.

Only Bad Girls Wear Stilettos

"**S**TILETTOS MAKE THE ORDINARY EXTRAORDINARY," I said to my niece. I had absolutely no data to support this, but on the fly it had seemed a decent theory.

My sister climbed from her daughter's Ford Explorer and stood to wait for me in the grocery store parking lot. In the truck with nineteen-year-old Emma, I kicked off my flip-flop sandals.

"Before your mom and I go into the store for ice cream, I'm going to put on a pair of the heels you've got stashed on the floor of your truck."

"Go ahead, Aunt Becky, but I think my shoes will be too big for you."

I started rummaging. Two pairs of Emma's towering heels were obscured in a pile of clothing she'd abandoned on the truck's floorboard. I selected a shoe from the top of a wrinkled assortment of skinny jeans, blouses, and miniskirts. I had to dig a little to locate its mate. I surfaced clutching a camouflage-patterned platform shoe

with a spiked heel. No, that wasn't the one I'd wanted. I sought a black shoe of identical style, with a gold studded ankle strap. By feel, I located my treasure, liberated it from the tangle, and slipped it on. My sister poked her head through the truck's open door and urged me to hurry.

"Becky, it's ten o'clock at night, and the parking lot is empty. Who's even going to see your shoes?"

"I'm planning to conjure some fun," I said. For some reason, I was confident I could do so.

I stepped from the truck and appraised my surroundings. I could see my sister's point. I thought of Dorothy, bedecked in ruby slippers, as she traversed the Land of Oz. Only tonight there'd be no clicking of heels. One tiny misstep would land me flat on my face.

Although the air was cool, I shed my black cardigan sweater and tossed it onto the backseat of the truck. I couldn't be expected to launch a swashbuckling adventure dressed like a middle-aged woman. I felt sexy in my body-tight dress and Emma's too-tall heels. I also felt grateful there was no full-length mirror on the premises. My accurate reflection might have spoiled the fun.

Midway to our destination, I resigned my futile attempt to keep pace with my sensibly soled sister. With the speed and focus of a woman on a mission, she'd covered the distance from the truck to the store's automatic door and passed on through. A good ten steps behind her, I teetered precariously. From the onset, my feet had slid uncomfortably forward into the toe-box of each shoe, which I had soon realized were not shoes in the least. They were twin torture chambers on stilts.

As I approached the storefront, three men in a canvas-top Jeep careened into the parking lot. As soon as they captured me in their high beams, they began to whoop and whistle in rowdy delight. Never one to disappoint, I raised both arms above my head, clasped my right hand over my left, swung my narrow hips in as womanly a fashion as I could muster, and sashayed through the store's automatic door. The men's robust cheers were silenced as the door slid shut. I panicked. What was I supposed to do now? I cried out to my sister in a frantic plea for backup support, but she did not reply. She had vanished into an expansive jungle of prepackaged food.

At the juncture of the freezer aisle and magazine rack I paused to regroup. Where was my sister? She was supposed to be right there, holding court with Ben & Jerry. I turned to face the rows of tabloids. Apparently Jennifer Aniston was pregnant. Under normal circumstances my curiosity would have demanded I soak up every false detail, but given that I'd just baited a Jeep of howling coyotes, Jen and her fetus would have to wait. I took a deep breath and smoothed my dress.

Suddenly, a stocky, bearded man in his midthirties approached me, wrapped his arm around my waist, and pulled me close.

"I saw you in the parking lot as we drove up," he said. "I *love* your shoes."

"Thank you. They belong to my niece."

"Do you and your sister want to drink wine with me and my buddies tonight?"

"How did you know we were sisters?"

"It's obvious."

Had I heard right? Had this he-man of a youngster implied that there were physical similarities between my bikini-contest-winning sister and *moi?* I flipped my hair. I stuck out my modest chest. My ego danced a jig.

"Well, she's married," I said.

"I don't care. Married doesn't mean you two can't come drink with us."

"I don't think my sister's husband would see it that way."

The young man freed me. I was relieved. In spite of my pompous charade, I'd felt uncomfortable awarding him too close a view of my wrinkles. Better to keep a distance. He stepped into a nearby checkout line to purchase the beer and wine his friends had deposited onto the conveyor belt. My sister reappeared. Thank God. We grabbed what we needed and headed to the checkout line where the fates had preceded us. We wound up directly behind the three men. My sister set down a carton of moose tracks ice cream and a jumbo-sized bottle of Hershey's chocolate syrup. She must've taken to mainlining the stuff.

I lowered my voice to a fervid whisper. "Where did you disappear to? I *needed* you."

"Becky, you're embarrassing! I was hiding behind an Oreo display halfway down the freezer aisle."

"I'm sorry, I guess. I don't know what got into me. I couldn't resist."

The guys finished their transaction, grabbed their twelve-pack of Corona by the inverted handle, and toted several bottles of wine. There was a dull clinking as the bottles fell inside the paper bag. The men faced my sister and me to exchange good-byes. Suddenly, I felt uncharacteristically shy, suffering from a dose of adventurer's remorse, perhaps. I had just ridden a wave of excitement that got me in over my head.

We thanked our suitors—not really coyotes after all—for their invitation to party. The men passed through the automatic door, climbed into their Jeep, and drove slowly from the lot. I was relieved to teeter back to the Explorer, where I returned the torture chambers to their rightful place amidst my niece's rumpled clothes. I collapsed into the backseat, pulled my safety harness across my chest, and slid my cramped and fevered feet into my flip-flops. Their surface was cool and welcoming.

In the past twelve months, I've been handcuffed by police, been approached by a gigolo, sipped tea with Christian Grey, and had my gynecologist ask me out following my exam. Oh, and an older married man from the track invited me to visit his home while his wife was at work. Am I somehow inviting these circumstances unintentionally? My family and friends offered their input—

"You're unguarded. Men interpret your outgoing nature as an invitation," said my sister Nina.

"You need to establish definite boundaries with men," said my writer friend Suzette.

"You're naive to think men don't want to have sex with you," said my workout buddy Elaine.

"In men's minds, a fun girl equals an easy girl," said my next-door neighbor.

"Wear longer skirts," said my eighty-year-old father. According to him, women in short skirts are floozies, and only bad girls wear stilettos.

Popular opinion thinks I should change. I should pull in on the reins. I should simmer down. I should be suspicious. I should guard against men's inappropriate behavior by altering *my* behavior, because evidently, men can't control themselves. This may be a case of "give 'em an inch and they'll take a mile."

There's one problem. I don't think I can squelch my personality for long, even if I tried. Altogether, I *like* myself this way. I see it as an asset that I readily give compliments, smile easily, exchange playful banter with acquaintances, and grab ahold of spontaneous adventure.

When a person is outgoing, they are apt to attract an abundance of attention, some good, some not so good. If a person is introverted or sullen, they will attract far less of both. My mother used to say: "You will catch more flies with honey than with vinegar." I have proven her right. I have caught my share of flies. But perhaps I can become more aware of the message my airy chutzpah might be communicating in some circles, and adjust accordingly. I could (possibly) simmer down a teensy bit as needed.

And, for the record, I think my father has it wrong. I believe it's untrue that only bad girls wear stilettos. Old girls wear them too. With similar results.

My 151st First Date

YOU CAN'T CHANGE THE BEAST. *You can only change yourself.* This had become my new mantra. I was determined to cure myself of gravitating toward the men I'd been habitually attracted to— charismatic commitment-phobes—because the men I'd been attracted to cannot be changed into the man I needed them to be: my husband.

I'd aim for a surer bet this time. Somebody who was understated and steadfast. A man who knew what he wanted, and was ready for what he wanted: a relationship with me. I would make a smart choice and select a man who could at least afford to buy me dinner. Match.com offered up Michael. He was my first date in five weeks. I hadn't been out with a man since my time with Zuri. And Garrett.

Michael's online photos were attractive. At fifty-three, he retained a boyish countenance and a full head of dark hair. He was short, but I've realized, *I can't have it all.* I understand this by now. Boy, do I understand it. Some people assume I'm single because I'm too picky. The truth is, I don't want to have it all, and I don't expect to have it all. I only want *enough.*

❧

Michael made reservations at upscale Café Fiore in Ventura. We planned to meet at six. I allowed myself plenty of time to drive the forty-five minutes from Santa Barbara to my destination. I ran late because I missed the Thompson Avenue exit and ended up in Oxnard. I pulled off the freeway to call Michael.

"Hi, Michael. I apologize, but I'm going to be late. You may as well know this about me, sometimes I daydream while I'm driving. I forget to pay attention to things like off-ramps. I'm getting back on the freeway headed north. I'll be there in about fifteen minutes."

He was nice about it. He said it was no problem. That's how I expected he would respond. Prior to our date, Michael had told me he prided himself on his "genteel" manners.

I arrived to the street where the restaurant was located, but I couldn't find parking out front. Finally, I parked on the fourth level of a nearby public garage. There was no elevator. I'd worn heels that hurt. I walked down four flights of stairs. I was glad I'd had my hair straightened at the salon earlier that day. Even with the evening's frantic change of pace, I remained confident that my hair looked fantastic.

Twenty-five minutes after I'd called Michael, I entered the restaurant. I found Michael sitting in the lounge sipping a glass of red wine. Not only was he short, he was plump. I pictured him on a rotisserie with an apple in his mouth. When Michael spoke he gestured with his hands: two stubby starfish that grew from his wrists. *I can't have it all.*

"Hello," he said. "We lost our reservation, so it may be a while before we get a table. Would you like a glass of wine?"

My nervousness spilled out of me in a rush. "I'm sorry about my lateness but I spaced out and I'm not familiar with this area and it was so hard to find parking—have you ever heard of a parking garage with no elevator?" I willed myself to slow down. "Yes, thank you, wine would be great." My feet ached. They wanted Uggs.

After ten minutes, the hostess seated us in a booth. I slid into the seat across from Michael.

"The proximity of the table to the seat reminds me of the safety bar on an amusement park ride—it's such a snug fit," he said. Michael blamed the booth, not his belly. In marked contrast, our booth had afforded me ample room. A *truly* snug fit is the backseat of a police car, but I knew better than to take our conversation there.

When I stood to go to the restroom, Michael stood too. "I like to honor a lady," he said. Though foreign to me, I thought his manners sweet.

Michael's Match.com profile had been well written—definitely above the norm. Although, the first time I read it, I'd found it slightly odd that a portion of his bio featured numbered paragraphs that stated the key components of a healthy relationship. He had capitalized on his online profile to expound his beliefs. He was trying too hard. Michael's bio lacked heart. But I shrugged it off. *I can't have it all.*

I returned from the restroom. Again, Michael stood, and remained standing, until I was seated. The second time around, I was slightly embarrassed by his over-the-top manners. *Sit down already!*

"I like to attend relationship seminars and workshops," said Michael. "Often, I'm one of the few men in attendance who isn't gay."

I laughed. Given some insight into the situation, it was all beginning to make sense. His relationship philosophy was directly patterned after what he'd learned in class. It was good, I supposed, that Michael was a man who was intentional about dating and commitment, but his

overall manner seemed contrived. I wondered if his "honoring a lady" line was something he'd picked up in class as well.

Michael slid his cloth napkin from beneath the tableware and placed it in his lap. A waiter approached, took our order, and left a basket of bread. My date slathered butter on a slice of warm sourdough and took a bite. His lips glistened with greasy residue.

"Modern women claim they want a relationship," said Michael, "but most of them are too caught up in their own independence. Independence has become their god. The Bible says a man will leave his father and mother and cleave to his wife. Women fear giving up their autonomy to join with a man." He positioned his elbows on the table and intertwined his starfish fingers—an illustration of a man and woman cleaving, I presumed. "A relationship is based on a choice, not a feeling," he said.

The waiter returned with our meals. I enjoyed my chicken ravioli with fresh mozzarella. I finished my glass of wine. I yawned. Above the din of restaurant conversation, I could detect my car's siren song beckoning me toward a speedy getaway.

"I agree with some of what you're saying, Michael. I frequently use the word *choice*—it's empowering. But I get the impression you're trying to sell me something. Your verbal delivery reminds me of a PowerPoint presentation, not a conversation, so it's difficult for me to connect with you. A woman needs to feel she *wants* to choose a relationship, not that she's being *pressured* to choose. People want to *buy* a product, not be *sold* a product." Never before had I been so candid on a first date.

He bristled. "I don't like the term 'PowerPoint.' It seems outdated and boring."

Boring, yes—I agreed. I suddenly remembered I needed to replace the brush head on my electric toothbrush.

"I don't mean to offend you, Michael. Maybe 'PowerPoint' isn't the right word. Falling in love is not an exact science, and that's why it's tricky. Love is not arrived at by making a determination, although choosing smart is—well—smart. Discovering romantic love at midlife requires a combination of chemistry and good judgment. It's an elusive butterfly." I was tempted to sing a few bars from the classic Glen Campbell riff.

The bill arrived on a plastic tray. Michael put down his credit card. I followed suit. I was certain he'd hand my card back to me. After all, he was *genteel*. But my credit card remained on the tab. "Thank you," he said. "This was just a meet-and-greet. If I had asked you on a real date, I'd pick up the entire tab."

Apparently calling to invite me to go to dinner at a restaurant where he'd made reservations did not qualify as a date. In spite of all his "women need to give up their autonomy" talk, Michael still believed a woman should carry her half of the bill. He'd said he liked to honor a lady, but his words were as cheap as his pocketbook.

We walked out together. California Street was brightly lit and bustling with the weekend crowd. I put on my jacket although the night was not cold; I hadn't wanted to carry it. Michael and I walked to the parking garage where we'd both left our cars. I was eager to leave. I began my ascent of the stairs.

"Thank you and have a good night!" I called to Michael. He started up the steps behind me.

"Don't worry, I'm not following you. I'm parked on the second level. I'm trying to act the true gentleman by seeing this date through."

I've always held to the belief that if a man is a true gentleman, it's not necessary he announce it. I rolled my eyes. If I was one to wear bangs, I would have stuck out my lower lip and blown a stream of exasperated air, lifting them slightly. Michael had gotten on my last nerve.

I drove home to my sweatpants and my Uggs and my independence. I replaced the brush head on my electric toothbrush. I brushed my teeth. I stared at myself in the bathroom mirror. *Why has it been so hard for me to find a decent man? How many more dates like tonight's will be required before I meet somebody suitable? Is there Häagen-Dazs in my freezer? If there is, I can have it all.*

I turned off the bathroom light and stood in the darkness. I listened. The refrigerator motor turned on. I heard a cricket outside. I switched on the light. I smiled at my reflection. Crow's-feet appeared at the corners of my eyes, and I noticed my mascara had smudged a little during the evening. My gloss had worn off and my lips felt uncomfortably dry. But my hair still looked fantastic.

A Second Chance to Say Good-bye

I'M NOT *ALWAYS* A SUCKER FOR THE CHARISMATIC, unavailable, or overinflated types. On one occasion I got things right. A year after I'd left my spouse and our family home, an unassuming old man with wasps in his attic—and a decrepit back porch—graciously opened his door to me. Without hesitation, I stepped over the threshold. Perhaps it was his bygone charm I was attracted to, and maybe it was my joyful acceptance of his aged character that endeared me to him. Our union was built on a crumbling foundation, but I didn't care. From the first, the elderly gent and me were reciprocally smitten. Old Man House was my safe haven.

Ninety-one years ago—in 1925—an eight-hundred-square-foot craftsman kit was delivered by boxcar to the San Luis Obispo train depot. The container held materials made to last: redwood, straight-grain fir, brick, gypsum board, and a cast-iron claw-foot bathtub.

A truck transported the freight to a nearby vacant lot. Like a multifaceted puzzle, the house was assembled piece by piece. The finished structure was a modest bungalow with an overhang front porch. The owner had spent a bundle on the tiny gem. The catalog purchase price: about $1,000.

Following my 2006 divorce, I bought the vintage fixer-upper for a *wee* more than a thousand bucks. During my seventeen-year marriage, I had co-owned several properties with my husband, but this was the first time I'd invested on my own. My ramshackle nest was located downtown near the locally famous High Street Deli. Each afternoon at 4:20 (code for cannabis), the deli offered a sandwich special. The double entendre was clever merchandising, the sandwiches, delicious. The neighborhood welcomed my children and me. Although our residence provided a too-snug fit for a family of five, it became home. We dubbed our wavy-windowed sloped-floor abode "Old Man House." I loved that little cottage up until I let it go. Honestly, I love it still.

At the close of escrow, I got busy. I ripped out shabby wall-to-wall carpets and extracted countless staples from the mahogany-stained fir floors. The exterminators showed up, tossed striped circus-like tents over the ridge beam, and battened them. Meanwhile, inside the house, my paint scraper and I ravaged aged linoleum cemented with black (asbestos infused?) glue. At the last minute—before poisonous gas was administered—a bug-killing professional escorted me to safety. Two days later, a floor installer arrived to lay bathroom and kitchen tile. The lady from next door dropped in bearing gifts: hot-from-the-oven apple turnovers—one for me, *two* for the hunky workman. I was a dervish with a paintbrush or roller. Previously drab rooms echoed with color. I painted the claw foot tub tangerine.

For six years I was queen of my castle. Neighbors would stop by to share remembrances of my home's curious past. At one time, a family of eight (six children!) had lived in my little cottage. A policeman had once resided there too. One night after the late shift, he retired to the living room to nurse a bottle of booze and clean his gun. The weapon misfired. The wayward bullet penetrated the living room wall and entered the front bedroom where his young daughter slept. The lead-tipped missile spared her by a hair. A benevolent spirit haunted my home's back bedroom. On occasion, I'd wake to the cloying scent of her perfume, which veiled my lower face like a surgeon's mask.

When it became necessary I sell, I staged my home with select pieces of furniture: our family's 1935 metal-topped dining table, rough-hewn coffee table, mission-style desk, pine kitchen hutch, and multicolored rag rugs. I applied Orange Oil to the timeworn floors, Soft Scrub to the tub, and Windex to the windows. My house sold. The buyers purchased the furniture I'd utilized for staging. By that time, two of my children lived across town with their father, and my daughter Nelly had married and relocated to Texas. Twelve-year-old Max and I settled ninety miles south in Santa Barbara. I lay in bed some nights and mentally wandered through my SLO bungalow. I missed Old Man House. I hadn't said a proper good-bye.

Two years passed. Nelly returned to San Luis Obispo when she was eight months pregnant. She'd made arrangements to give birth at the hospital where her daughter had been born four years before. Nelly's husband stayed behind in Texas. Stationed at Fort Hood, he planned to fly out when his wife was ready to deliver. Nelly's plans to lodge with family fell through. She and daughter Pearl had nowhere to stay. I suggested she search Craigslist for a thirty-day rental. I agreed to cover expenses. She soon discovered that short-term leases in San Luis Obispo were rare.

A day later, Nelly phoned. "Mom, your little house is a vacation rental! I've contacted the owners and they've promised to lease it to me for thirty days!"

Who said you can never go home again?

Nelly and Pearl moved their suitcases in. Max and I drove up to visit on weekends. For the most part, Old Man House had remained the same. At meal times, we selected our plates and bowls from the familiar pine hutch. Pearl ate lunch at the metal-topped table where my kids ate when they were small. She bathed in the antique tangerine tub.

After I'd sold my bungalow and moved away, the two-story house next door acquired new landscaping. The dew-laden lawn I once traipsed across to arrive at Tarek's front door had withered and died, and had been replaced with drought-tolerant plants. Our longstanding tryst had come to an end, and Tarek graduated university and relocated, but surprisingly, the entry's rickety wooden steps had remained intact. Whenever Pearl and I passed the yellow house on our morning walks, I gave it wide berth and averted my eyes. The memories enshrined in the spicy recesses called to me, but I did not resurrect them. My impish granddaughter and I chased monarchs instead.

My son-in-law arrived from Texas. Beneath the overhang front porch where I'd once carved gap-toothed jack-o'-lanterns, Pearl's daddy carved one just for her. At bedtime, I bunked with the benevolent spirit. My daughter gave birth at Sierra Vista Hospital. She and her husband brought their baby home to Old Man House.

Thirty days passed too quickly. The time came for us to say good-bye to each other and bid farewell to our former abode. I made certain I was the last to exit. I walked from one room to the next and whispered my thanks to the structure that had served as my fortress and sanctuary during the difficult years that followed my divorce. I thanked my little craftsman bungalow for sheltering my daughter's young family. I expressed gratefulness that I'd been granted the opportunity to draw close to my beloved home one last time.

With a voice steeped in impatience, Nelly called to me from the front doorway. "Hurry up, Mom! We've got to get going!" I broke from the elderly gent's protective embrace and stepped across the threshold into the October sunshine. Pearl's jack-o'-lantern grinned from its porch-side perch. My daughter locked the house behind her, and then we drove away.

My friend Liv is a hospice volunteer. Her experience with the dying has taught her that life's "little let-gos"—a job loss, a hopelessly lost pet, a broken heart, declining health—prepare us for the eventual "big let-go": death. That makes sense. *Still,* I've recognized that sometimes life—and love—will require we let go, give up, and move on, but then—miraculously—when we least expect it, something I define as *grace* will circle back around, offering us a second chance at life, love, or saying good-bye.

I've a Crush

I've a crush.

I'm vexed. Smitten. Moonstruck.

My heart's aflutter—a Luna Moth—alive in the night.

I long for the magic to linger but I accept it will be fleeting.

I won't struggle against impermanence.

Struggle brings turmoil.

Turmoil is not welcome here.

A crush is best not trifled with.

Mine will go no further than the initial pleasure it brings.

He's unaware he's hung the moon.

I will leave him in the dark.

To savor my secret is prize enough.

I've a crush.

Trimmings

DICKENS'S SCROOGE HAS NOTHING ON ME. My favorite day of the year? January 2: the winter holidays are officially over.

When my kids were little, the holidays were enjoyable because I knew it was fun for *them*. But even back then, I could only weather so much. Oven roasting a turkey was an overwhelming chore. My then-husband Mickey would barbeque one instead. On the morning of December 26, I'd remove the ornaments and lights from our family's Christmas tree, lug the parched pine outside, and then vacuum. Perhaps my aversion to Christmas has impacted my older kids, but not fourteen-year-old Max. Max *loves* Christmas. He watches Christmas movies on his iPad in July.

My sisters live out of town. My older children are spread out; two live with their father, and daughter Nelly is married and resides in Texas. It's not surprising that Max prefers to spend Thanksgiving and Christmas with his dad. Mickey celebrates in a traditional manner, and Max craves his holiday fix. So, ever since my mom's death in 2012, it's just my eighty-year-old father and me for the holidays. For the time being, I don't mind this arrangement. I *adore* my father.

Plus, I don't have a fella I'm sweet on to spend the holidays with. I'm in what Wall Street refers to as a "quiet period": a duration where I'm not actively promoting myself. This Thanksgiving my Pops made dinner reservations at a Santa Barbara landmark: Harry's Plaza Cafe. For the occasion, I gussied up.

I pulled my wet-from-the-shower hair into a sleek ponytail and secured it with a black elastic band and a generous dollop of styling gel. I placed another elastic band at the end of my ponytail to subdue the unruly curls that would inevitably revolt once my mane began to dry. Then, I applied my makeup: a light powder foundation, bronzer, mascara, a smudge of eyeliner, and coral-hued lipstick. I put on my favorite pair of earrings: glass cobalt beads attached to silver wires. Next, I dressed in an above-the-knee black knit skirt, a latte-colored blouse, and stylish but sensible black heels with ankle straps. Before I stepped into the night, I donned a buttery black leather jacket. I drove to my father's house. I knew he'd be sitting in his recliner, waiting.

"You look nice," said Pops. His compliment was kind, but it lacked pizazz. I'd hoped for "Holy smoke, daughter! You're gorgeous!" But no such luck.

"Thank you," I said. "Tonight, I'm your arm candy."

Harry's Plaza Cafe reflects a bygone era. It carries an elegant but tawdry ambiance reminiscent of an old-time brothel. The walls are embellished with damask wallpaper obscured by a multitude of framed celebrity photos. Red leaded-glass fixtures hang from the red ceiling. The deep booths are upholstered in vinyl button tuck—red, of course. Harry's offers a menu specializing in comfort food: fish and chips, roast beef or turkey dip sandwiches, and spaghetti and meatballs. But the eatery is famous for its cocktails. Every drink is a double.

Our reservation was for 5:30. We arrived at five o'clock. My father is always early. Unfortunately, I've not inherited his early-bird gene. It must be recessive. We stood in the foyer and waited to check in with the hostess. I looked around at my surroundings. The place was hoppin'. Apparently I wasn't the only one who'd no interest in roasting a turkey with all the trimmings. I focused on my reflection in the entryway mirror. Amid the restaurant hubbub, time stopped. I stood and stared—transfixed. My outfit looked sharp, but when had my neck become a series of vertical cords? When had subtle jowls encroached upon the corners of my mouth? Had I not been in public, I would've positioned the forefinger of each hand on opposite cheekbones and pulled upward—momentarily erasing the signs of age.

The hostess assured us that our table would be ready shortly. Until then, Pops and I volunteered to sit at the polished stretch of bar. We bellied up. I sat on a red vinyl-topped stool next to a man in his late forties with wholesome farm-boy looks. He wore Levis, a cotton button-down shirt, and a baseball cap. Nothing about his appearance bowled me over. *A good sign,* I thought.

We exchanged introductions. Neil tipped his cap and commented on the football game televised above the bar. *He's the type of guy you should go for, Rebecca. A nice normal dude. A little shy, maybe, a diamond in the rough, perhaps; a man who doesn't call attention to himself—a sleeper.*

Neil repeatedly looked in my direction but I felt awkward engaging him. I would've included my father, but his hearing is impaired. There was no way my dad could participate in a three-way conversation inside a noisy restaurant. Besides, there was the crux of the matter: at age fifty-seven, I still sought his approval. I didn't want to take the risk that Pops would label me a floozy. I didn't speak with

Neil because I was afraid my father would peg me a desperate woman who hits on guys at bars. I ordered a glass of pinot noir. Pops, a gin and tonic: his favorite.

I sat across from my father in a button-tuck booth. My wine had cast its mellow spell and I relaxed into the moment. Pops nursed his gin and tonic. He spread butter on a slice of sourdough and took a bite. The years have been kind to him. He's retained a full head of hair—now lustrous silver. He has deep-set gray-blue eyes, and a full, handsome face free of wrinkles. Twenty-five years ago, my dad was a fire captain for the city of Santa Barbara. Male firefighters in Santa Barbara are unusually attractive. I choose to believe my father set the standard. Pops finished his bread and smiled. His teeth are white and gorgeous, strong and straight. Unlike mine, they'd never required orthodontia.

Neil's unexpected appearance at our table cut short my daddy worship.

"I'm taking off, but I wanted to wish you both a Happy Thanksgiving."

"Thank you, Neil. Happy Thanksgiving to you too!" I said.

My father and Neil shook hands; then Neil walked away.

"He was pretty brave to come over to say good-bye," said my father. "I think he wanted to ask you out."

"No, he didn't. If he'd wanted to, he would have."

On this point, I was confident the bigwig dating experts would back me up.

"It's intimidating for a guy to ask a woman out when she's sitting with her father."

"You're right, Pops. But I don't think it was my place to offer my number when Neil didn't ask. What do *you* think I should've done?"

At ages nineteen and twenty, my parents tied the knot and

remained happily married for fifty-eight years. When my mom died of Parkinson's my father lost the love of his life. He still refers to her as his bride. As a young bachelor, he'd had limited time to be a ladies' man. He'd never experienced the highs and lows of long-term single life. But regardless, Pops has acquired the knack for bestowing sound dating advice.

"You handled yourself well, but it's too bad Neil didn't ask you out."

Obviously, my concerns over my father's harsh judgment were unfounded.

I looked to my eighty-year-old dad for salve-like wisdom that would restore the lost opportunity with Neil.

"What can I do about it now?" I asked.

My father took a sip of his gin and tonic. His face was flushed with the effects of its medicinal magic.

"You can get over it and move on."

I laughed. It's clear that Pops has a bright future as a swami or a dating coach.

Our waitress approached. I ordered spaghetti and meatballs. My father selected the traditional Thanksgiving meal: oven-roasted turkey with all the trimmings.

Grateful for Small Mercies

EACH MORNING, MY INTERNAL ALARM CLOCK WAKES ME five minutes before sunlight slips between the slats of the living room window's vertical blinds and projects its rays onto the adjacent wall. Max has taken over our apartment's only bedroom. He's a teenager. He requires his own space—his own bedroom door to slam. The living room is my space. At bedtime, I wrap myself in a patchwork quilt and sleep alone on the couch.

Within a span of nine years I've experienced a surplus of dating adventures. I've made my share of dating debacles, and I've celebrated my share of successes. I have given midlife dating my best effort, and I've not conceded to defeat—even when my heart has been trampled and my ego lay exposed like a fragile, powder-blue robin's egg.

I had supposed Mr. Right would be in my life by the time I finished writing this book. I imagined the last chapter of my collection would be a proclamation of my dating triumph, an encouragement to single middle-aged women everywhere: if I can do it, you can too! I anticipated introducing my hard-earned man-prize to you, fair reader, and including a photo of us together. Yet, at the completion of my manuscript, I've acquired not a man, but a perspective.

I've arrived at a destination point of sorts. I have come into a mindful awareness of *knowing*, in my bones, the characteristics of the man I'm looking for:

He will be emotionally available and marriage minded; before we are lovers we'll be in love.

He will abstain from whiskey and watermelon gum—at least simultaneously. He will prefer kissing girls to boys, and drink two beers at one sitting—not twelve. He'll flash a spontaneous smile as he pours me a glass of wine out on his leaf-littered, coyote-haunted patio. I'll be his Valentine.

He will listen and consider what I say. He'll call instead of text. A good-natured ribbing will not deter him—he'll playfully volley back.

He will enjoy steady and satisfying employment, mix metals with clueless abandon, and drive a vehicle that is compact and sporty—incapable of sleeping six. He will be a member of the 56 percent who are open to dating an older woman, even if I happen to be his junior. He'll shake my dad's hand, then ask me out. His openness will distinguish him. His receptivity will score him the winning point.

I will not be equal in years to Mr. Right's mother. On date number one, he'll not suggest we split the check. He will be admiring should I wear stilettos or shimmery stockings, yet appreciate me in jeans and flip-flops. When we go out, his beanie will stay home.

He'll stand with me—whether I'm handcuffed on State Street, or elsewhere.

He'll be convinced that Pollyanna-me is just his cup of tea. He'll collect bold, vibrant art. His "junk" will not be available for hire. His name may well be Bernie or Harold or Eugene—and I will shout it from the rooftop.

We'll choose love over fear. He'll be my safe haven.

Dorothy's ruby slippers possessed no greater magic than my niece's stilettos. It's never the shoes that create the adventure, but the one who wears them.

For nearly a decade, I ran with the man-bulls and I ran strong. But nobody can maintain that pace forever. I've grown weary of my search for love. I've grown tired of the striving as well as the disappointment. I have considered retiring from cyberspace dating, and maybe I will. Or maybe I'll hang in there, but go on fewer dates.

I now entertain the possibility that dating at fever pitch is not a prerequisite for finding love at midlife, as I'd once thought. If that's the case, maybe I should relax a little. Perhaps I'll kick off my high-heeled ankle boots for good and adopt a more comfortable stride, while remaining open to the intrigue of *amour*. Because, in spite of life's discouraging circumstances, I remain buoyed by the scope of its possibilities. If my dating experiences have taught me anything, it's to expect the unexpected.

And to be grateful for small mercies:

The nocturnal beckoning of a young lover. The kindness of strangers when I ventured out alone. Wine on a rustic wharf above the bright Pacific. The solace of driving home after a bad date. Dressing to look my best. Conversation over a midday cup of tea. Breaking one hundred.

For laughing with abandon—and crying in heartbroken agony.

For feeling alive.

I'm grateful to have been unceremoniously dumped by one guy so I'd be free to kiss another.

I attended a Catholic Mass hoping to encounter a man who'd love me, but instead, God met me there. I've discovered that my earthly father is a pretty cool date.

I have learned to savor a clandestine crush, and to move on from heartache without rancor. I've grown up some.

I've yet to achieve my goal of discovering authentic love at midlife. Yet, even though many of my suitors have been a mismatch, I believe my compulsion to seek love hasn't been misdirected, misfortunate, or a mistake.

I harbor no regrets.

In the end, my dating episodes have led me to realize that I'm capable, resilient, complete, and *happy* as I am.

With or without a man.

The Complete Idioms' Guide to Online Dating @ Midlife

(Accredited by the School of Hard Knocks)

A T THIS STAGE OF MY LIFE, online dating has proven itself an
excellent teacher, although not a lenient taskmaster. Modeled
after commonsense idioms, I leave you with lessons I've learned
along the way:

- **Seize the day.** It's easy to do nothing. It's easy to make
  excuses for *why* you don't have a healthy love relationship.
  Excuses require no time, effort, or risk. Neither do excuses
  provide an opportunity for success. Hooray! You've decided
  to be proactive with your love life. You've planned to stop
  doing nothing and start looking for Mr. Right.

- **Cast your nets.** (Not to be confused with *castanets*.) Utilize your options. Subscribe to more than one dating site. Doing so will increase the number of men you're exposed to and will distract you from placing too much emphasis on the productivity of one specific site. You will eventually discover which online sites work best for you.

- **Be a smart cookie.** Compose the best-written profile you can. Ask a friend with writing skills to help if you need it. But above all—be honest. Attempting to make yourself appear taller, thinner, or younger than you are will invariably backfire when you meet your dates. Don't assume a gracious suitor will overlook your "little white lies" once he has met you. *Nobody* tolerates a little white liar.

- **Smile from ear to ear.** Accompany your written profile with at least five current, quality photos. Refrain from posting only head shots. A man wants to see the entire you. Be aware that your provocative photos will attract a lot of attention— from old geezer perverts. Don't post pics of lovely scenery, or your pets and children, unless you're in the photos, too. Men do not join a dating site to romance a sunset, a flower, or a kitten.

- **It's only a matter of time.** Invest fifteen to thirty minutes a day on your dating accounts. It's to your benefit that male members see you are active. If you don't log on to your account for weeks, your profile will sit stagnant. Sometimes I'll log on to a dating site with the intention of contacting one new man. Even minimal activity helps keep one's cyber-juices flowing.

- **Touch base.** Match.com supplies its members the option to "Wink," "Favorite," or "Like" a subscriber's photo. Plenty Of Fish members can "Send a Flirt," "Favorite," or scroll through the "Meet Me" lineup. These are methods subscribers utilize to contact one another if they choose not to send an email. I may forward a noncommittal *wink* to a man I'm ambivalent about. If he responds, I may consider him more seriously. I suppose men wink at me for similar reasons. Email exchange between members usually signals a level of greater interest.

- **No fraidy-cats!** Occasionally I'll come across a disclaimer attached to a man's profile that threatens legal action should anybody "steal" material from his bio. Theoretically, "profile pirates" *could* create fake profiles from legitimate ones in order to promote a scam—though in reality, this is rare. When an individual attaches a hostile warning to their profile, their fear of being taken advantage of is what stands out. No matter how polished their profile, it's their paranoia that has made a lasting impression. Dating sites should exist as venues of good will—not suspicion. A public proclamation of mistrust regarding the site one has subscribed to is counterproductive.

- **Pretty is as pretty does.** Let's face it: the exceedingly beautiful people don't need our attention. They get their due. Invest your charm elsewhere. Unless you're one of the beautiful people. In that case, go for it. Exceedingly beautiful people need love too.

- **Stick close to home.** Cyber-mates can be introduced from anywhere in the world. Some individuals claim they are willing to commute or relocate to be with the one they love. Very romantic. Yet, if your match lives miles from you, the pragmatic prognosis for dating success is slim. Local relationships are hard. Out-of-town relationships are harder. Consider before you embark on long-distance love, long-distance phone bills, and long-distance heartache.

- **Don't rob the cradle.** To snatch a babe from his bed has its perks. I appreciate a much younger man for his enthusiasm, openness, physical beauty, and . . . his youth! Young(er) men are delightful. Yet consider: perhaps Junior adores your adoration of him, but entertains no plans beyond his present satisfaction. I wouldn't squelch a middle-aged woman's desire to drink from her suitor's virile fountain of youth, *but* she should be realistic about the eventual outcome, be true to her relationship goals, and proceed with caution.

- **Keep a low profile.** Do not log on to a dating site on Friday or Saturday nights, or major holidays. I understand you are home. Alone. Again. Yet *he* doesn't need to know that. Who, you ask, cares about what some proverbial "he" may think? Understood. But if you want to be an effective online dater, play it cool. Cool is beneficial. Cool is your new best friend.

- **Boys will be boys.** Men write the darnedest things! I believe most middle-aged males who subscribe to dating sites are decent guys who've had little experience wooing the fairer sex online. After reading thousands of profiles, I've discovered that men seek similar traits in a romantic partner: a low-maintenance drama-free motorcycle-mama who cooks in the bedroom as well as the kitchen, *and* is willing to exercise her criminal tendencies. The following profile is a composite of many I've encountered online—

Hello, ladies. I'm just an average guy with no baggage (not even a carry-on! Lol!). I'm the real deal. I'm also better looking than my photos. Lol! I live, laugh, and love because life is too short for drama—or rap. I enjoy a variety of outdoor activities like camping at the lake, beach walks, or riding my Harley. I enjoy indoor activities too, such as watching a movie or cuddling in front of a fire with someone special. Speaking of sex, I love sex. Just being honest! Lol! I seek my best friend and partner in crime. She'll be a woman who goes from a T-shirt and jeans to a little black dress in 15 minutes and looks fantastic. Bonus points if you can cook! Lol! Shoot me an email. XOXO

- **Make a long story short.** When an attractive/interesting man emails you, reply to him in a positive yet concise manner. I enjoy the art of correspondence. I enjoy it so much that I've made the mistake of responding to men's brief emails with lengthy commentaries. No more. I've discovered it's best to keep one's emails short and sweet. "Hello, I love you!" takes my suggestion too far.

- **Courtesy costs nothing.** If a man from a dating site writes you a thoughtful email, answer him. If you're unsure what constitutes a "thoughtful email," here's an example:

Hello rockymtnhighness,
I've had the pleasure of reading your profile and reviewing your photos. I think you and I may have several things in common. Please take a look at my profile to see if you agree. I hope to hear from you. –David

If you are not interested in David, reply anyway. It is the kind and conscientious thing to do, as well as an opportunity for you to set the bar for online dating etiquette. If I'm not interested in a man who's sent me a thoughtful email, I'll send the following:

Hi David,

Although I don't think I'm the best match for you, I do appreciate the nice attention you've sent my way. My sincere best wishes to you on your search. ~rockymtnhighness

- **Don't buckle.** Once in a while, a man may press to inquire *why* you have "rejected" him. You are not obligated to explain yourself. You have already informed him you're not interested. If he chooses to belabor the point, that's *his* problem, not yours. Should his emails turn into harassment, notify the dating site and block him from messaging you. He'll move on to somebody else.

- **Pull the devil by the tail.** On occasion, be reckless! Email all the too-hot guys your heart desires. Email ten men who are ten years your junior. Email only men who make $150,000+. The worst you will suffer is a mild dose of post-email embarrassment. Who knows what fun (or success) you might conjure up?

- **Hold the phone.** *"Hellooo?"* Your phone number should not be a party favor gifted to all men in attendance. Refrain from offering your number until a man requests it. If an online contact solicits your phone number or personal email address too soon, be suspicious. You are never obligated to share. Do not ask for a man's number. He'll give it freely if he's interested.

- **Take the plunge.** Get off the chaise lounge and jump into the dating pool! Prolonged email correspondence or numerous phone conversations are *not* reliable indicators of attraction or compatibility. Emails and phone chats are no substitute for a face-to-face encounter.

- **Don't jump the gun.** When a man you're interested in asks you out, say, "Yes!" but refrain from moving things along too fast. Agree to meet him in a public place for coffee, tea, or one glass of wine. I've learned the hard way that meeting a first-time date for dinner may trap me in an uncomfortable scenario for too long.

  I'd agreed to meet a man who'd driven two hours to treat me to a lavish meal. Although he was pleasant, the commute time alone was enough to be a deal-breaker. The man had purchased dinner and drinks, and then gifted me a bottle of wine as we'd said good-bye. I'd felt guilty eating the dinner he'd paid for. I'd felt guilty accepting the bottle of wine he'd proffered me. I'd not known how to refuse his generosity without causing bruised feelings. I've heard it said that men enjoy the act of giving to a woman. I think that's true *if* the woman reciprocates his affections. Otherwise, a man may feel he's been used. It's best to keep first-time dates brief and inexpensive. Sometimes I don't follow my own advice—*and I have regretted it.*

- **Cut a fine figure.** Don't try too hard, nor too little, to impress. When you go on a date, dress appropriately for the planned activity. Always show up as yourself, but as your *best* self. Never resort to Christmas tree earrings.

- **Don't put all your eggs in one basket.** I've heard it said: if you give a man ten women, he'll play; if you give a woman ten men, she'll choose. In the initial meet-and-greet stage of a romantic relationship, it's wise that a woman date multiple men, so she will not build unrealistic expectations toward one specific man too soon. This is common sense, yet it's difficult for me to follow. When I find a man I like, I like *him*. If our connection dissolves, I'll require a few days to recover before I get back in the game. I've always been a one-basket woman.

- **Give it a shot.** One of the drawbacks of meeting men online is the pressure we put on ourselves to make a hasty decision about whether or not they meet our standards. If you sense a man has potential, go out with him several times. A healthy connection does not happen overnight. All authentic relationships grow slowly over time. When I meet a man for a first date, I experience a profound sense of relief when there's even a *hint* of mutual attraction. A hint of attraction has the potential for growth. Growth potential is favorable to no potential, and growth potential is favorable to fireworks. My friend the therapist says: "When a woman feels romantic fireworks on a first date, she should run." We women do run, but generally it's toward the explosion.

- **Don't bust his chops.** He told you he would call at 5:30. He called at 7:30. He was ten minutes late for your first date. He doesn't open the car door for you. When he does not act as you had anticipated he should, cut him some slack. Is he an evil person, or has he experienced an atypical bout of male-pattern cluelessness? That is for you to determine over time, not on your first date.

- **Don't chase him down.** I'm a sunflower type rather than a wallflower. I go after what I want. This trait does not transfer well to romance. Whenever I've chased a man, it has *never* worked in my favor. *If* a man is interested in me, he will pursue. *But if he doesn't know I exist, how can he pursue me?* Sometimes I'll initiate contact by emailing a man a brief hello. If he doesn't respond, I have my answer. If he does respond, I have my in!

- **I kid you not.** Conventional wisdom tells us our kids should not be exposed to their single parent's love life. I partially agree. I think our children should not be exposed to their parent's *sex* life, but casual friendships with the opposite sex are part of reality. I never hide my male friendships from my fourteen-year-old son. I encourage him to make friends with his peers, and I believe it's healthy for him to see that I have friends too. My son knows I go on dates, but nowadays, I *always* come home alone.

- **Zip it!** *You have the right to remain silent!* Refrain from sharing too much too soon. If a new man asks why I adopted, I'm not obligated to go into detail. It is preferable I not. A new suitor doesn't need to know I'd had a chlamydia infection that blocked my fallopian tubes. *Too much information!* While engaged in a getting-to-know-you chat, steer clear of the word "infection."

- **Don't drink like a fish.** You're anxious about meeting a handsome man for a drink. A glass of wine or a beer will

help you to relax. Stop at one drink. Do not order another. On a first date, you want to present yourself as an alluring butterfly, not a sloppy barfly.

- **Don't count your chickens before they hatch.** To paraphrase martial artist Bruce Lee: *When you think you have found the way, you have lost the way.* Everything changes. Nothing remains the same. Anything can, and *will,* happen online. I've had men contact me and ask me out, and then suddenly cancel their dating site subscription, never to be heard from again. I've had men write me numerous thoughtful emails but never initiate a date. One man gave me a passionate goodnight kiss but didn't ask me out again. Nothing is a sure thing until it is.

- **Err on the side of caution.** Fifty-five-year-old Andy is still randy. Middle-aged men desire sex as much as men decades younger, though perhaps not as often. Don't assume an older man will have your best interest at heart just because he's "mature." *You* are in charge of your own welfare. Make sound judgments. All middle-aged men I've had sex with preferred to forgo condoms. In moments of sexual reverie, I've acquiesced to such tomfoolery. Only later, after the man had dropped off the face of the earth, did I worry which STD he'd gifted me. Such unnecessary suffering! Get tested for STDs. Insist your partner be tested too. Have sex with him *after* he has asked you to be exclusive. Solid advice from a prude.

- **Hang in there.** Most men that you encounter on Internet sites will *not* be your suitable matches. Most men you encounter in "real life" will not become your lovers. It is infrequent that one will meet another with whom they fit.

Each day we come into contact with countless individuals. How many of those do we hope to see again? It's rare when we discover a man that we long to stand beside, share conversation with, touch, or kiss. It's best to approach online dating with a positive outlook and few preconceived expectations. To maintain an open, patient, and relaxed attitude requires practice. And wine.

- **You're the bee's knees.** Should a woman text her date (*Thx 4 the fun!*) when she has arrived home? I think it's a polite gesture. Especially if she'd like to see him again. Yet the hard truth is this: if a man wants another date, he will usually ask me *before* we've parted ways. If he doesn't inquire, it's a clear indication he doesn't want to go out again. When it comes to being rejected, I've taught myself to be philosophical: *he wasn't meant for me*; and pragmatic: *I want a man who digs me, not a man who doesn't.*

- **Let the chips fall where they may.** It does absolutely no good to obsess over what you cannot control. You cannot make a man love you. You cannot make a man treat you well. You can control only two things: your words and your actions. Own them.

- **Read the writing on the wall.** It would be inspiring to lay bare a new man's closet and unearth no skeletons. But if skeletons are found—even *one*—I've learned it's not in my best interest to feign ignorance, but to face reality and take action. It's foolish to assume a suitor's deep-seated issues or preferences will suddenly dissipate by miracle or magic. His words and actions demonstrate who he is. For better or worse, *believe him.*

- **Keep the faith.** I've compared my search for Mr. Right to a crowded parking garage with all the parking spaces taken. How many parking spaces are required for me to park my car? You're right! Only one. As I drive around and around the garage, I wait for a space to open up. I'm confident that if I keep circling the garage, my turn will come. Eventually it does, and I park my car, as nice as pie. Likewise, I don't require scores of eligible men to open up to me. I require only one man, as nice as pie.

- **Walk on.** Your ex was a jerk. Your last date didn't go as you'd hoped. Nor did the date before that. Do not let "bad" men or "bad" circumstances determine your attitude towards a *new* guy. One disappointing turn does not automatically lead to another. Each man is a unique individual and is not responsible for your past heartache. No matter what awaits you around the bend, *keep moving forward.* Baby steps count.

- **Tell him to scram!** You *always* have the option to walk away. If the man you've begun dating does not love you and treat you well, break it off. Find a man who will hold your hand during your colonoscopy.

- **A bird in the hand is worth two in the bush.** Online dating sites offer (too) many opportunities to discover one's love match. There will *always* be one more profile to read, and *always* one more email in your inbox. It's simply the nature of online dating. When you've discovered a man who's a "keeper," hide your profile (after he hides his), and invest your time building a relationship. First, pinch yourself!

- **Have the patience of Job.** These things take time. You can't hurry love.

Acknowledgments

*C*OMPETENT: HAVING THE NECESSARY ABILITY, knowledge, or skill to do something successfully.

Kind: having or showing a friendly, generous, and considerate nature.

Long-suffering: long and patient endurance.

I've come to understand why authors rave about their editors. Jamye Shelleby Doerfler is competent, kind, and long-suffering. She took on my shabby first draft, and my determination to learn, and taught me how to write a book. I could not have written *Miss Matched at Midlife* without Jamye in my corner.

Dr. Keith Witt's foreword started *Miss Matched at Midlife* with a bang.

As promised, publisher North Loop Books has created a stellar product. Author coordinator Ali McManamon runs a tight ship. Kate Ankofski is an editorial sommelier. Formatter C. Tramell made my book's interior look like art.

Friendship: harmony, accord, understanding, and rapport.

Frank and Jeri Wascoe listened with sincere interest from the time of my book's inception. Their candid and constructive feedback from the readers' perspective has proven invaluable.

Judy Katz (creator of ghostbooksters.com) shared her long-standing literary experience. Judy was a part of the trusted circle of early readers who afforded her expert assessment—and praise—as *Miss Matched at Midlife* took shape.

Marjorie Garland, Carol Maxwell, Jackie Lincoln, and Santa Barbara Matchmaker Lisa Amador have been my loyal cheerleaders.

Family: stuck together by circumstances and love.

My father, Charles W. Brockway Jr., has been a willing ear and (brawny) shoulder of support. Not once did my pragmatic Pops remind me how difficult it is for an emerging author to achieve success. The words he *didn't* say were as uplifting as the words he did say.

My cousin David Amack offered a single middle-aged man's perspective on *Miss Matched at Midlife.* David's editorial and technology skills helped me revise awkward sentence structure and decode the mysteries of my website.

Although my children are on the fence about their mother's newfound passion for writing, I hope my accomplishment has made them proud.

Suitor: a man who courts a woman to earn her favor.

To the men I've dated and loved (as well as those I didn't even like): unbeknownst to you, you've gifted me life lessons—delights *and* disappointments—that are priceless. Under your tutelage, I've matured and emerged as the savvy woman I am today.